BODY
Intelligence

BODY
Intelligence

HOW TO "THINK"
OUTSIDE YOUR BRAIN

JOHN MAYFIELD, D.C

nu
BALANCE

GRASS VALLEY, CALIFORNIA
nubalancepublishing.com

Nubalance Publishing Company
Grass Valley, California

Copyright © 2009 by John Mayfield

ISBN 978-0-9884937-2-8

Library of Congress Control Number 2008911637

Printed in the United States of America
10 9 8 7 6 5 4 3 2 1 first edition

Library of Congress Cataloging-in-Publication Data
Mayfield, John.
Body Intelligence: How to "Think" Outside of Your Brain / John Mayfield
1. Mind and body. 2. Vitality. 3. Breathing. 4. Posture.
5. Healing. 6. Holistic Medicine 7. Spirituality

Publisher: Judy Mayfield
Editors: Taran March and Adam Heilbrun
Proofreader: Terry Vaughan
Layout: David Hurst
Cover Design: Kimberly Nelson

CONTENTS

Acknowledgments

I have often heard the saying "it takes a village to raise a child." I discovered it also takes a village to write a book. I especially want to thank my beautiful wife who spent so much of her time meticulously editing the painfully awful first drafts, and all of the edits and re-writes. Most of all I want to thank her for the continuing love and support, and her undaunted optimism throughout the process of my becoming a writer.

I offer my heartfelt thanks to all of my patients for their participation in the process of learning and practicing these healing principles. Over the years, working with all of you has allowed me to refine the way I talk about these concepts, and later to write about them. I also want to thank Katrina Morris, Jennifer Crebbin, and Tom Wilson for their insights and clarity. I sincerely appreciate the patience and kindness of Dr. Jeffrey Kaufman who gave so much of his valuable time reviewing the five elements.

I especially want to thank writers and dear friends, James and Wenda O'Reilly and cover artist Kimberly Nelson for the three intensive weeks it took to brainstorm the front and back book cover and for the strategic changes that made the book more accessible to readers.

And finally I want to give thanks to editors Taran March and Adam Heilbrun, proofreading by Terry Vaughan, formatting by David Hurst, and my brother and best friend, Jim Mayfield, who would haul me off to the ski slopes when I got wound too tight to think straight.

Oceans

I have a feeling that my boat has struck,
down in the depths, against a great thing.
And nothing happens!
Nothing . . . Silence . . . Waves . . .
Nothing happens? Or has everything happened,
and are we standing now, quietly
in the new life?

—Juan Ramon Jimenez

The Eloquence of Being Human:
A Healer's Perspective

We are living in interesting times. With each passing day, we are increasingly aware that our inner world is more important than the world out there. Your body is intelligent. Every part of your body is like a polygraph that exhibits distress when you are not in alignment with your deepest sense of truth, love, and decisiveness.

Healing is a process of discovery. By the time you have healed yourself, you will have discovered that you do not have a body and a separate mind. You have a *bodymind*. Each part of your body is a part of your total consciousness. You cannot separate physical, mental, or emotional health from spiritual health. They are all one.

We are awakening to the notion that what we focus on is precisely what we create in our lives. We each manifest our own personal reality. Then we live in it. However, without tools for understanding this concept, the mind can seem as vast as the fathomless, trackless ocean must have seemed to early explorers.

Now is the time for each of us to take control of our own thoughts and emotional realities. This is a new day, and each one of us must change the way we look at it. What we pay attention to is what we become conscious of, and we each create our own unique world by what we choose to focus our attention upon.

As an individual, you are the dreamer who has always dreamed your world into being. You have always had the freedom to focus your attention on whatever you choose. The consequence of your focus is the world you have manifested into being. You have always had free will to create your own personal reality within the context of what is going on around you.

Abdominal Breathing
THE FIRST SIMPLE HABIT
THAT WILL CHANGE YOUR LIFE

After slumbering for millennia, we have developed patterns of inertia that are difficult to overcome. The inertia makes it difficult to go from unconsciousness to full awareness. You might remember from physics that "an object at rest tends to stay at rest."

Because of the inertia, awakening requires tools. *Abdominal breathing is the first gate of heaven.*[1] It is a clear pathway to higher consciousness. Until you learn to breathe properly, it is the most important habit you will ever undertake.

Each time you catch yourself breathing shallowly and resume breathing out forcefully from your lower abdomen, you awaken from the spell of time. Each moment of awakening is an opportunity to realize that this moment is the answer to all your prayers and desires. It has no history, only potential.

Each time you take a few cleansing breaths (fast deep breath) and begin to breathe out forcefully from your lower abdomen you awaken from a spell. "Spell" is a perfect word because these are old dysfunctional programs that project the past or the future over this moment. You are drawn back into these old programs, over and over, until you replace them. Each act of resuming abdominal breathing eliminates one more old unconscious program and replaces it with a new default program.

---

1 Chapters 1 through 14, and Chapter 43 discuss breathing, the first habit that will change your life.

As you replace old unconscious programs with more aware ones, your self-esteem steadily increases. When you breathe abdominally it gives you the energy to accomplish your splendid plans.

Everyone falls asleep—that is, becomes unaware—many times a day. Falling asleep is not the issue. Waking up is what's important. Each time you fall asleep, your body's response is to immediately start breathing shallowly. You go into a spell. Your rational, fear-based mind takes over and plunges you into the world of time.

Each time you start breathing in and out forcefully from your lower abdomen you awaken to the here and now. In the present moment there is no fear or guilt; there are only choices and consequences that you, a spiritual being, make. As a spiritual being, you are unconditionally loved and completely safe.

Posture of Awareness
THE SECOND SIMPLE HABIT
THAT WILL CHANGE YOUR LIFE

Correct posture has no past history, so it is not a vessel for holding pain or suffering in our bodies.[2] It is not constantly influencing us into some artificial construct of an imagined future with all its fears and worries. Most people's posture and gait are continually, one step at a time, reproducing their total history of pain and suffering. Because correct posture has no history, it naturally brings us back into the present moment.

---

2   Chapters 15 through 27 reveal the importance of posture.

Posture is the second gate of heaven. Heaven and hell exist right here. Every slumping posture or way of favoring an injury becomes a vessel that holds a vast library of fear and guilt, pain and suffering. The moment you slump, you find yourself languishing in the seventh circle of hell. Your rational mind loads some old story that overlays the moment with past memories about how hard you must work or how hard you have it, and you are drawn back into the spell of time. We all have thousands of these programs.

Shake it off. Stand up into good posture, and you immediately wake up from the spell. In good posture there is no history. There is only the here and now. Your spirit's natural state is bliss, and it naturally bubbles up to the surface when you are awake and relaxed.

Standing erect presents a commanding presence. Each posture you emulate is actually an instruction to others, telling them how you want them to respond to you. When your head is thrust forward, out there in the future, you are saying, "Respond to me later." You probably mean now. That posture forces you to live in the future. It is like dangling a carrot in front of a donkey. In this case, the instruction you are giving yourself is: "Everything will be good when I . . . "

There is no traction in the past or the future. "Give me a long enough lever, and a place to stand," said Archimedes, "and I can move the world." The place to stand is now, here—this moment. With good posture, you are present. You are in the moment. In the "I am" moment, you transcend the limitations of your past and the implicit fears regarding the future.

In this moment your only limitations are the boundaries of your imagination. "What you can conceive and believe, you can achieve."[3] The trouble is that you must be awake to fully access your imagination.

Your body and spirit are like a horse and rider, respectively. When your physical body, with its rational mind, eagerly submits to your spirit-rider's control, the whole universe becomes your playground. You wind up getting your deepest desires.

3 Hill, Napoleon. *Think and Grow Rich.* (Ballantine Books, 1987.)

Walk Away from Your Injuries
Like a Cat

THE THIRD SIMPLE HABIT
THAT WILL CHANGE YOUR LIFE

There is a big difference between dogs and cats in the way they relate to injuries. Most dogs are like people. They favor their injuries. They milk an injury for all it is worth.[4]

Favoring an injury is an unconscious act. Essentially, it is giving your power away. There are many postural ways of giving our power away, like slumping when you are around shorter individuals. In the unconscious state, people assume postures that show the world that they are not who they want to be.

The trouble is, when you favor an injury, you start to think of it as something permanent in your body. You add one injury at a time into your repertoire. Then with each step, each movement you replicate that injury. The injuries become part of your history. People go so far as to give their injuries names, "My bad knee; or my (pick an illness)." Cats demonstrate a better way.

Cats, who spend most of their time outdoors, move with a whole body awareness, which keeps them in present time awareness. When you move like that, you retain the simple pleasure of movement. Every part of your body communicates clearly with every other part of your body.

Cats heal fast. They do not squander their life force limping, gimping or favoring an injury. Their consciousness is laser focused in the present moment. They do not linger in self-pity. For them, the past, even if it is only one second ago, is past.

---

4   Chapters 15 through 18 deal with the big difference between dogs and cats in the way they relate to injuries.

Developing whole body awareness is a habit one can acquire, like standing erect, moving with good posture, forcefully breathing out from your lower abdomen, lifting up your buttocks when you walk. The more physically aware you are, the more spiritually awake you are. Physical and spiritual awareness may not be the same thing, but they walk side-by-side down the same path.

Feel Your Feelings
INSTEAD OF POPPING INTO YOUR BRAIN'S RATIONALIZATIONS ABOUT YOUR FEELINGS

Feeling your feelings is the fourth simple habit that will change your life.[5] All through history people have intellectualized their feelings instead of going inside and actually feeling their feelings. They say things like, "I am so disappointed in Bob or Sue," but they do not actually feel the disappointment.

You can talk about your anger or other feeling you are having until you get a number of knots in your rope, but all you are doing is rationalizing. Intellectualizing your feelings only strengthens the problem. This does not lead to soul growth. Spiritually, it is called sleepwalking.

Your emotional energies and your spirit's energies are very similar. They both fill all of the space around you. You can feel when someone loves you—or despises you. You can feel when someone wants something from you. The energy of people's feelings is palpable. You access your spiritual wisdom by asking yourself leading questions about feelings you have, especially when you have feelings that do not represent how you want to create your unique world.

---

5   This is covered in depth on pages 3, 15 through 17 and Chapters 44, 45 and 46.

The wisdom of your spirit is latent unless you have tools to access it. You want to question your feelings, like an aggressive reporter would, to get to the wisdom of your spirit. The answers come freely, in your own voice, but their source is your spirit. The wisdom is always there, but you need better questions to get at it.

Other tools to access your spirit's wisdom begin with trust. Trust, wisdom, respect, power in the manifest world and all oneness are the five chakras (energy centers) of your spiritual body.[6] They simply are. You do not have to earn them. You have never lost them. You just may need to shine them up a little. Trust the process. Trust that the source of all that is conspires to give you all that your heart desires. The more you can learn to trust, the better your life becomes.

Listen to Your "First Feelings" in New Situations
TO ACCESS YOUR BODYMIND WISDOM

This is the fifth habit[7] that will change your life. It is so easy to go unconscious. All of us do it numerous times each day. We need habits that goad us into waking up. Learning to be aware of your first feelings (about anything) is one of those habits. Your first feeling is your innate intuition.

Practice being aware of your first feeling when you walk into a new situation. Everything sharpens up. You feel alive. How you handle the situation replaces another dysfunctional program. This is the conscious way to live.

6   Bartholomew, "I Come as a Brother" (Hay House, 1997.)
7   Discussed on pages 42, 43, 152 and 154

But, if all of your awareness is on what is going on outside of yourself, then you are so distracted that your rational mind takes over. Ignoring your first feeling is the mechanism that allows you to go unconscious. Then your rational mind takes you back to the earliest time you were unsuccessful relative to that particular feeling. It overlays your unresolved emotional response from that time period over this event, and you become "the six year old that does not fit in" or any other of thousands of unresolved response patterns.

This is the transcendent mechanism that facilitates healing old emotional traumas. The painful way you respond to similar events keeps reoccurring until you finally get it. Your mind never shirks from its transcendent job of throwing any unresolved emotional pattern back in your face until you do get it.

When you go inside and feel your feeling, you replace that old unresolved memory with the new one that you are handling more consciously. If not, your mind keeps reliving your old painful unresolved feelings, over and over until you consciously feel them. Isn't that a great way to learn? Pain is your friend.

Your first impression of a new person you meet is how you will feel about this person when you have enough experiences to know them well. I had a very smart dog that taught me this. It took me a long time to figure out how she could always tell the good guys from the bad guys—every time. I finally figured out that she never negated her first feelings. Simple.

Cherish Others

This is the sixth simple habit that will change your life.[8] As part of the "five elements," you learn in detail that your heart is the emperor of your unique world. Cherishing yourself and others, and cherishing your splendid plans and dreams is the ultimate purpose of your life.

All through grade school, high school and college we have been taught that our brain drives the car. Well it does, but only in the unconscious state. When your rational mind is in control of what you consider reality to be, you live in the world of time.

Twenty-five hundred years ago the Buddha realized that believing the past or the future has any control over you is the cause of all pain and suffering. He called it the realm of all unsatisfactoriness. Every spiritual teacher throughout time has echoed this truth.

When we wake up, we realize that it is our heart that truly controls our world. Love is the only vehicle worthy of riding in.

Act.
Be Decisive. Make Things Happen
IT'S BETTER TO MAKE MISTAKES
THAN TO DO NOTHING

This seventh simple habit[9] changes your world. Creation is simple, not complex. Truth is simple. Each one of your seven-dimensional bodies has to react instantaneously to whatever you are doing. Since all of your subtle bodies occupy the same space at the same time, each one of them has very simple operating systems.

---

8 Discussed in Chapters 33 through 37
9 Discussed on pages 47, 48 and 107, and Chapters 47 through 52)

Every part of your body and mind, or more accurately bodymind, is like an extremely accurate polygraph. Any part of your consciousness that is not in truth goes into dis-ease. Even though your body always does the best it can, dis-ease, over time, can become disease. What you think, feel and believe is the main issue of your body's health.

The basis of your character is like a triangle that you stand upon, and hopefully keep in balance. Each point of your triangle is supportive of the other two foundations of your reality. Rudolf Steiner called the three points heart, mind and will.[10] Heart is cherishing yourself, cherishing others and cherishing your plans and dreams.

Mind is being honorable, telling the truth, walking your talk. Mind is also realizing that your heart is the emperor and putting your thoughts in abeyance to your heart. When your mind thinks it is in charge, you are back in the world of time with all of its pain and suffering.

Will is the third equal point of the triangle that makes up your character. Will is about being decisive—taking action. When you are indecisive, you negate your truth. You cheapen your love. Basically, the wheels fall off your car. Acting on your desires and your truths is every bit as essential to who you are as telling the truth and cherishing others.

It is far better to make mistakes, even big ones, than to do nothing. This is how we learn. The greatest among us have openly admitted that they failed their way toward success. You can do a thousand things right and learn very little about life or about yourself. Do one thing really stupid or mean spirited (and be reflective about it) and you learn an immense amount. If you are paying attention and learning from your mistakes, then it is all good.

When you withhold your truth by not deciding, you steal from your loved ones. It takes courage to say what you believe, to do what you deeply want to do, but it is the only life worth living.

10 Rudolph Steiner developed Waldorf education and a system of philosophy called anthroposophy (science of spirit).

Every person needs to put his piece into the puzzle that is life. Any person that does not put his piece in leaves a glaring hole in the puzzle. Each person has her particular genius, and the world needs that genius quality if it is to be whole. We all need your contribution.

The Five Elements
THE BASIS OF TRADITIONAL
CHINESE THOUGHT

The "five elements"[11] are so many things to so many people. To me the elements of wood, fire, earth, metal and water represent the five separate and unique channels through which we comprehend the world around us. The unique way each person interprets this information becomes the basis of consciousness.

Wood represents the way you perceive the structure of your world. It is like the frame of the house you live in. Your liver is the architect of all that makes up your life and the world you perceive. Your gall bladder functions as the general contractor that turns all of the liver's plans into tangible structures and realities. It makes all of the short and long-range decisions about the liver's plans. It makes good judgments, which the liver relies upon to plan efficiently.

Fire represents all of the expressions of love that bind every aspect of the universe together. Every social interchange has love as its basis. As we awaken, we become more inclusive and more people are allowed to come to the table and share their gifts and talents. In the unconscious state we are more exclusive. We make rules that keep others from affecting us. All of the exclusionary policies and laws become obstacles that dissipate at least seventy percent of the energies each of us must expend in our efforts to make a living. We could be cherishing others and including them. Instead, we must work about nine months out of every year just to deal with the obstacles our fear-based policies create.

11 Discussed in Chapters 29 through 46

All of your cells and organs look to your heart the way you might imagine the source of all that is. Your heart is your personal connection with divinity. All of your thoughts, feelings, attitudes and beliefs are your subjects. They are your heart's to command. Take command of them. If you do not, someone else will. The few that have steadfastly refused to let others define their realities have been the heroes of prior ages. A heretic of one age can become a sage of the next.

All of the other elements exist within the element of earth. Earth, within your consciousness, represents all of the ways that you accept (or reject) the bounty that is all around you. It is the nurturing way you get the sweetness out of life. Earth is the original archetype of mother. It is through this element that you learn physical and social boundaries and develop your sense of distribution.

The element of metal is the archetype of father. It is through this part of your consciousness that you learn trust, respect, wisdom, power in the manifest world and all oneness. You come to see your intrinsic value through the element of metal in much the same way that you assign value to precious metals and gemstones. Metal, like the molten core at the center of earth, is the fire in your belly.

Water represents your feelings. It is your connection to spirit. Through the element of water you learn endurance, the strength to carry on through hardship, and the ability to survive year after year. Healthy water reservoirs ensure that you have a future. Water gives your mind the fluidity that allows thoughts and ideas to flow.

Water gives you the season of winter when the earth is replenished with life-giving water. It is a time to look within and wonder about your deep abiding values, whether you are aligned with those values. Through this element you learn to forgive, to release old painful hurts. The wisdom of the element of water teaches you to always confront all of your fears—and move on.

Your kidneys[12] are actually intuitive brains. The logic of your rational mind gets caught up in the historical world of time. Your kidney's first feeling gives you an exact preview of how you are going to feel later.

Freedom is the fruit of self-discipline. Isn't that an interesting enigma? By contrast, the more that people try to be free, the more encumbered they become. Make a mental list of people you know who are the most free in their lives. Then notice how disciplined they are.

The habits discussed in this book help you to live at the upper limits of life. My desire is for you to live the good life. When you are focusing your awareness on what you love and showering your splendid plans and dreams with loving feelings, your heart is developing insights that help you manifest more of what you love into your life. This is a far better strategy than focusing on all of the problems around you, which forces your heart to develop insights into how you can create more problems in your life.

The habit of making the world a better place gives you the most profound sense of fullfillment. The more positively focused you become, the progressively greater your life becomes. The better it goes, the better it gets. Age empowers you, and your life keeps becoming better than you ever thought it could be.

As I reflect back, every part of my life has followed a path toward understanding and demystifying the way our bodies, minds, and spirits interface. The great surprise for me has been a progressive realization of how simple our operating laws are—how elegantly simple and rewarding it is to live in the upper limits of this life.

I have lived with the habits I have described in this book and taught them to my patients over the years. These habits have become the foundation of my healing and continue to make my life and the lives of my patients richer beyond anything I could have ever imagined. I wish you a rich experience of life. There is so much more goodness waiting for all of us to discover.

12 Discussed on page 154

CHAPTER 1

The Inner Journey of Breath

Breathing out forcefully from your lower abdomen is your first gate to heaven on earth. This habit will change your life profoundly. Each time you catch yourself breathing shallowly and then resume breathing abdominally, you awaken from the spell of historical time—the world of past, with its regrets, or the future, with its fears. *Breathing in is passive. It happens all by itself.*

A few deep breaths, and you step out of the quagmire of historical time. The present moment you awaken to is quite literally the answer to all of your prayers and desires.

You ever-more consciously become the lead actor in the unfolding drama of your life. You take the first step of your odyssey when you breathe enough oxygen to fuel your magnificent plans and splendid dreams.

Life joins in and contributes ten steps for every one you invest. Becoming the lead actor in your life's unfolding drama requires a mere ten percent of the energy required to make it happen. For every step you take, ten steps are added to your effort.

Breath as Life

Imagine this scenario: A man's breath caught in the top of his throat. A bolt of fear running down his spine. He feels steel rods running down his legs, deep into the earth, freezing his feet to the ground. He wants to run but cannot move a muscle. Brain-numbing, freezing-your-feet fear is excitement without the breath needed to back it up.

People have performed superhuman feats during times of danger, when they knew they had to, especially when the danger was to their loved ones. When a dangerous situation suddenly arises, your mind goes into a full adrenaline hyperdrive. Time slows way down. Within microseconds you analyze the danger (which might normally require minutes to analyze). You hear yourself saying *"No!"* to the dangerous outcome you know will happen if you do not act.

The instant you say no, your adrenal glands kick full on to an extremely high level of intensity. You respond to the situation with phenomenal clarity and speed. The power that surges through your body is awesome. You save the day!

You breathe so powerfully in adrenaline-charged moments. Your commitment and mental clarity (the instantaneous, completely accurate appraisal) allow you to handle the situation better than you ever have in the past.

During times of danger, people exhibit varying responses. The adrenaline rush is common to everyone. How you handle it directly depends upon the level of your commitment. If you fail to commit, your rational mind goes into denial that the situation is happening, or that you have the power to do anything about it.

Your breath stops when you accept a situation as fate. When your breath starts again, it is extremely shallow. That kind of shallow breathing is what animals do when they think a predator is near; if they do not breathe, the predator will not hear or see them. These adrenaline rushes are extraordinary events, which you may or may not respond well to.

Dozens of times each day in your everyday world, you get into less intense situations that you handle well—or not so well. The determining factor of how you handle any of them is how you breathe. If your breath shrinks away, your courage to master the situation also diminishes.

Breathing abdominally gives you the fuel to live up to your full potential. When you breathe enough oxygen so all your cells have the stamina, power, and clarity they need, then you naturally possess the energy and confidence to seize the moment.

Your body requires large amounts of oxygen to courageously face up to everyday challenges. To meet and exceed life's challenges requires courage and stamina. Courage must be fueled.

If you want to pull off the big life, you must breathe deeply enough to get oxygen out to the furthest extremities: your fingertips, toes, and your brain.

When you know that you do not have enough stamina to meet and exceed the challenge in front of you, fear steps forward. Courage steps back. Your mind comes up with excuses instead of commitment.

When you breathe shallowly, fear and anxieties crowd you into living a smaller life than you would like. Your fears are the bars on your prison cell. Most fears are small ones like shyness or not wanting to appear pushy, or wondering what others might think. Emotional fears like frustration or worry follow directly on the heels of shallow breathing. Anxiety is excitement without the breath.[1]

---

1 Psychologist and writer Gay Hendricks, from his workshops.

We take breathing for granted. Everyone breathes, right? Well, everyone must at least breathe enough air to not die. Unfortunately, that is about how much air most people breathe—just enough to not die.

Breathing is the single most important factor affecting the quality of your life. And yet, you can live your entire life without giving breathing a second thought unless you get a condition like asthma or the wind knocked out of you.

In the five elements theory, which is the essence of acupuncture, your lungs represent your physical body's will to live, your right to be here. Owning your right to exist is defined as your animal spirit. All animals possess the will to live.

The life force of your animal spirit changes from moment to moment depending upon how much air you breathe (or don't breathe). The power of your animal spirit is a dynamic, constantly changing reality. You can be as awesome as a grizzly bear or as timid as a mouse. How much air you breathe determines whether you rise to the occasion or shrink from it.

I notice that every time I start walking anywhere—going out to my car, getting out of it, standing in the check-out line—I practice breathing out forcefully from my lower abdomen. Who I am, beyond all of the stories, comes into sharp relief.

Breathing Out
from Your Lower Abdomen

Breathing out from your lower abdomen gives you enough oxygen to live large. It is simple and effective. The more you belly-breathe, the more powerful your life becomes, the greater your total awareness becomes. This is a powerful tool.

When you breathe out from your lower abdomen, your diaphragm domes upward. As you relax, your diaphragm muscles involuntarily pull downward in a bowl shape. This creates a bellows action that powerfully pulls oxygen down into your lungs. Every cell in your body gets fully oxygenated.

Breathe this way any time you start to walk somewhere, when you find yourself standing in line, whenever the traffic stops, when you are sitting at your desk. It makes everything right as rain. All of your faculties come full on. You are totally alert. You want to breathe this way every time you think about it. The more you do, the better your entire body feels.

Breathe like this for a while. You fully energize your whole body—all the way to your fingertips and toes. You fully oxygenate your entire brain. Your thinking sharpens up. Your attention span becomes more laser-like. Your mental stamina allows you to embrace the big picture. You can wrap your mind around complex issues. You are living your dreams—making them happen.

When you breathe shallowly, life-giving oxygen barely gets out past your elbows or knees, much less to your fingertips and toes. That is one of the major reasons people have cold hands and feet. If your fingertips are not getting enough oxygen, what do you think is happening to that other extremity called your brain? Low energy is one of the simple secrets of stupidity.

Your brain and nervous system are your body's largest consumers of oxygen. Mental stamina requires a lot of oxygen. You really have to breathe abdominally to fuel mental endurance. When you breathe shallowly, it is difficult for you to imagine doing brilliant things, much less accomplishing your splendid plans and dreams.

If you are only breathing in enough fuel to accomplish a small life, it is extremely difficult to accomplish much more. Without adequate breath, you cannot see yourself in the picture of living the life of your dreams. Big breath fuels a big life. Shallow breathing crowds you into a little life. That's how simple it is.

When you begin breathing abdominally, it is easiest to imagine drawing your naval in each time you breathe out. Then you can increase your effectiveness by shifting your focus to two finger-widths below your naval.

CHAPTER 2

Hara

Hara is your one-point center. This is the center of your balance, and it is your place of power. Its location is two finger-widths below your naval and straight back to the front of your spine (fourth lumbar vertebra). That is your second-to-the-bottom vertebra.

In Japan, people are traditionally taught that *hara* is the one-point center of your balance and the epicenter of your awareness. In China, this same place of power is called *tang tien*.

Hara is where your spirit lives. It is the ancient heart place of your spirit. When your spirit aligns in *hara*, you feel your entire body simultaneously. Body-centered awareness is synonymous with spiritual awareness. You are being rather than thinking. You are living more in the moment. *Hara* is your singular place of power within your body.

When you breathe out from your lower abdomen, your spirit is drawn down into its proper home. You are fully incarnated. Your spirit has the same basic shape as your physical body. When your spirit is centered, every part of your spirit is aligned with the analogous parts of your body. That allows every part of your spirit to communicate with all the dimensions of your seven-dimensional physical body. Neither your body nor your spirit functions as well independently as they do together.

You feel more connected with your intuition. The more you trust it, the keener it grows. You feel your connection to the elemental world of nature. Plants and trees have an emotional life as full as yours. All of nature desires to communicate with you.

Traditionally, people growing up in Japan have a large number of sayings that focus their awareness into *hara*. If a child is being problematic, his parent might tell him that he has black *hara*. If the child is not doing what he or she has committed to, the parent might blame this on his or her weak *hara*. You do not want to be accused of having weak *hara*, because that is also the definition of a liar.

If a man commits to helping you on a certain date, he might clench his fist in front of *hara* as he says, "I will be there." That is like saying, "I commit my soul to helping you on that date." In America you are more likely to hear, "Call me to remind me." That's a lot different, isn't it? The results are different, too.

Your spirit has a focal point. It is about the size of a golf ball. It is the most energetic point in your body. If you have never given it much thought—and most Westerners have not—you probably have no idea where the focal point of your spirit resides.

To discover where your spirit is focused within your body, pause for a few seconds. *Use your imagination.* In your imagination there is no right or wrong. There is only what *you* experience.

○ Go inside of your body.
○ Close your eyes.
○ Notice the single place in your body where you are aware of feeling the most energy. Notice the place in your body where your awareness is drawn.
○ The part of your body where you experience the most energy is where you keep the focal point of your spirit.
○ Where you feel the most energy dictates, to a large degree, how you will experience your world.

Most Europeans and Americans focus their consciousness just above their eyes. If you focus your awareness up in your head, your perspective of reality will be limited to the mental realm. Having your rational mind dominate your viewpoint of reality is the opposite of spiritual awareness, or body-centered awareness.

Because we tend to keep the focal point of our spirits up in our heads, Western culture, as a whole, worships at the altar of rational thinking. Intuition becomes the bastard stepchild. Our dominant paradigm is excessively mental. We tend to "think" our reality.

When a culture is predominantly mental, judgments and rules become the dominant descriptors in their value systems. Respect for all life and the importance of being in balance with nature get nudged further into the background. Most of the value systems are based on objects or concepts outside of ourselves, rather than inner-directed values.

In our culture's preoccupation with mental values, we lose the intimate feeling of interconnectedness with other humans and the rest of the world. Our tendency is to dominate instead of resonate with the elemental world of nature.

When your awareness is focused up there in your head, everything gets a mental spin. Politics get reduced to polarized perspectives. Each side talks *at* each other. We come to the table with the principle aim of fighting for our own perspective, instead of coming from the more evolved desire to truly cooperate with each other, to help others get what they want while simultaneously asking for what we want.

When you are stuck in the world of time, spirituality loses its deep sense of personal connection. Instead, it descends into rigid rules that, if not met, separate you from others. The trouble is, those same rules, when not met, also separate you from your source. This is the fruit of living in your head.

When you have an "*ah-ha!*" moment, *hara* is the location in your body where you get it, where you own a truth. When you know something in your guts, then you've got it. *Hara* is where you commit to that truth. Knowing something in *hara* is a quantum leap beyond thinking it up there between your ears.

CHAPTER 3

Are You Awake?

When I was in the army (drafted during the late 1960s), I went to the tiny little library at the post where I was stationed to find a book to read. As I was looking at the dismally small selection, a book literally fell off the shelf. It fell into my hand.

A book falling into your hands is one of those auspicious power moments. The title of the book was *Hatha Yoga for Americans* by Indra Devi. This was not the kind of book I was looking to read. I wanted an action book. But, it did fall into my hands . . .

I decided to at least give it a once over. I randomly opened the book to a page that said in bold letters:

UNTIL YOU LEARN TO BREATHE PROPERLY,
BREATHING ABDOMINALLY
IS THE MOST IMPORTANT DISCIPLINE
YOU WILL EVER TAKE ON.

I was skeptical about the veracity of that statement and whether I even wanted to take on a discipline, but I read further. An illustration of the lungs showed how the diaphragm muscle performs as the floor of your bell-shaped lungs. When you breathe out, your abdominal muscles tighten inward toward *hara*. That pushes your diaphragm upward like a dome.

Mechanically, your lungs are passive. They are like sponges. By themselves, they cannot breathe. When you breathe out, it pushes your diaphragm upward into a dome, which compresses your lungs against the sidewalls of the bell-shaped rib cage. That squishes maximum amounts of carbon dioxide out of your lungs.

1 Devi, Indra. *Hatha Yoga for Americans.* (Prentice Hall, 1959.)

Your diaphragm has two muscles (on either side of your stomach) that reach down and attach to the fourth lumbar vertebra (*hara*). *Relaxing your abdominal muscles after forcefully breathing out signals those two muscles to tighten, which pulls your diaphragm downward like a bowl.*

Let's do a recap:

❍ Breathing in is passive.

❍ You tighten your lower abdominal muscles to forcefully breathe out.

❍ When you relax at the end of breathing out, the diaphragm muscles on either side of your stomach automatically tighten, which pulls the floor of your lungs downward into a bowl shape.

❍ This bellows action gives you the energy to accomplish your magnificent dreams.

Chest Breathing

The book went on to say, if your collarbones go up and down with each breath, you are a chest breather. Chest breathing is the least efficient way to breathe. Only the top three or four ribs exert any action on your lungs. That expands and contracts only the smallest part of your lungs. The lower two-thirds of the lungs do not work at all when you chest breathe. Bad form.

There was a little mirror on the wall of the library. I stood in front of the mirror and breathed my normal way. My collarbones went up and down with every breath. Shallow breathing was a puny way to breathe, but what I was doing was far worse. That got my attention. I checked the book out of the library.

Naturally, I began observing the way people around me breathed. The book stated that shallow breathing and especially chest breathing allowed your neurotic fears to come forward and take center stage in your life. Once your fears take center stage, they exert a lot of control over how you see the world. Fear dictates the way you see your world and the actions you take.

I could see that breathing shallowly nailed my feet to the ground because fears and anxieties held center stage. When I inwardly knew that I did not have enough breath energy to get the job done, fear became my advisor. That's how it works.

In the absence of enough energy to accomplish your goals or dreams, courage withers. It just fades away. Fear, which is lack of courage, fills in the void. Nature abhors a vacuum.

I began breathing abdominally. I did not know at that time how powerfully life-affirming that decision was. I just knew that breathing in such a puny amount of air filled my life with fears. Those fears stood in the way of the life I wanted to take hold of. Breathing abdominally sends down taproots that go deep into the soil of life.

For the first nine months, every time I checked in on myself, I was breathing shallowly. A few cleansing breaths woke me up. They also pulled me right out of a spell. Cleansing breaths, which are two or three fast, deep breaths, are pattern interrupters. They break you out of low-grade negative emotions.

Every time I came out of one of these spells, abdominal breathing gave me enough energy to replace the negative feeling with a successful outcome. Each successful outcome began to build my self-esteem. By the time nine months rolled around, I was breathing abdominally most of the time. By the end of the year, I was an abdominal breather.

Any major discipline has a gestational period. The time it takes to birth a new discipline is about the same amount of time it takes to have a baby. For the first nine months, every time you check in on yourself, you probably will be breathing shallowly. After about nine months, when you check in on yourself, most of the time you will be performing the discipline. By the end of a year, you can say, "I breathe abdominally."

CHAPTER 4

Internalizing Trauma

You do not have to let trauma be a part of your body. Beginning to breathe shallowly is the first step to anchoring a trauma into your physical body. Letting your posture start to slump is the next step.

Then you begin resonating with foreign thoughts that do not represent your truth. Accepting thoughts that are not how you want to create your world makes your mental body become unstable. Truth starts to slide down that slippery slope. Your mind sets up rationalizations to explain away the loss of integrity. The rationalizations take you out of the moment. You have left the garden. You are in the world of time.

Making the decision that you cannot handle certain feelings internalizes the emotional trauma into your body. Every part of your body is like an accurate polygraph. Whenever you encounter a similar or matching issue, any part of your body that is not in truth phases out of awareness. Your mind superimposes rationalizations over what you are seeing.

You change what you believe because of the trauma. Then your dreams become separate from you. You think, "I can't have that dream." Or, "Oh! That's impossible." Rationalizations are fear-based. They replace the simple truth that you are the dreamer who dreams your world into being. You forget that the whole universe exists so that (all) beings can evolve and get what they desire.

One at a time you allow your emotions, your thoughts, your breath, and your posture to accept the trauma as part of your body's makeup. The trauma becomes part of you. This is how you internalize trauma into your body.

You begin to breathe shallowly the instant you weave a rationalization into what you are observing. By default you let go of truth—and you lose the ability to create your world.

Most people are still unconscious. They choose by default. Immediately after you have an injury, there are pain and limitations. But when the pain lets up, we are not taught to take our power back. The truth is, our culture encourages us to practice hundreds of ingenious ways of giving our power away. We teach them to our children.

Giving power away is endemic throughout most of the world. Breathing out from your lower abdomen is a great tool for breaking out of those unconscious patterns we have all been socialized into for millennia.

You will want to practice breathing out forcefully as a beginning place for anything that is important to you. This is your first step to reclaiming your power—the first of the simple habits that will profoundly change your life.

CHAPTER 5

The Nature of Unconscious States

Each unconscious state originates with a particular negative emotion, or a positive emotion onto which we have attached a lot of negative baggage. The negative emotions are usually subtle, like worry, feeling some kind of lack, guilt, or fear. The emotion might be a deep, indescribable need (compulsion) to do something, or it might be boredom, frustration, lack, or anger.

Your rational mind retains all of your unresolved memories regarding things in your life where you attached negative feelings. A similar negative feeling will have an electrical charge in the library of your mind.

When you encounter a situation that triggers one of your unresolved memories and you do not pause to feel that feeling, the emotional charge engages your rational mind. Your rational mind does a lightening-fast search to the earliest time you felt that way.

Your mind immediately starts weaving a story. Its purpose is to tie that highly charged time to this situation. Emotionally, you have regressed to the age you were when you had that unresolved memory. You are no longer present in the moment. You are unconscious. As soon as you go unconscious, you start breathing shallowly. You revert into a posture that accurately reflects the way you felt at that earlier time. The whole gestalt floods in on you.

Not pausing to feel your feelings is the trigger. When a feeling comes up and you do not pause to feel it, that is the instant your rational mind takes over. The story your mind makes up enables you to rationalize that it is all right for you to indulge those feelings.

The story your mind makes up either inflates or diminishes yourself or the other person(s). Your rational mind weaves a plausible story about why you are indulging that feeling. That way you can stay asleep. You can keep on indulging that feeling.

No matter what your unconscious response is, the feeling you have is like being caught up in a spell. A spell is the best definition of these emotional states.

Shadow Issues

Each one of us has thousands of these old, unresolved emotional states. Psychologists call them "shadow issues." They do not exist in present time. They pull you into the shadowy realms of the past or future. Most of your shadow issues originated during early childhood or some traumatic time period. Once you fall into one of these spells, your coping skills correspond to the emotional age of the spell you are caught up in. Emotionally, you are that seven-year-old.

Your entire being is transcendent. You have a built-in mechanism that constantly seeks to transcend from unconsciousness to a state of awareness. "Transcendent" does not mean that you are automatically transported into a higher state of mind. In a holistic system, the exact opposite occurs.

Your body is holistic. Every one of its functions has feedback mechanisms. *The nature of feedback mechanisms regarding shadow issues is that you must keep coming back to the painful memory until you resolve it.*

Let's do a recap:

○ The moment you ignore your body's first feeling, you start breathing shallowly.

○ Your rational mind is immediately drawn back to the earliest time you felt that way.

○ The negative emotional charge is what draws your mind back into the memory.

○ That unresolved feeling is then projected over the top of the current scene. Because this is how the vast majority yet live, it appears normal.

○ To the degree that you are unconscious, the rationalization will dictate how you perceive and react to this scene.

○ Technically, you are not here. You are caught up in a spell. The spell transports you into the artificial realm of time.

You are compelled to return to your tired, old shadow issues as many times as it takes until you resolve them. That is the beauty of this innate healing mechanism. You are nudged in the direction of healing by having your painful issues thrown back into your face until you consciously choose to replace them. Pain is your friend.

Your shadow issues affect all the ways you move, think, feel, and believe. They distort your golf swing. They bring up all the fears that inhibit your magnificent plans and dreams. Shadow issues are all of the places in your consciousness where you phase out of awareness. In sports, anywhere you phase out of awareness shows up as flaws in your technique: your golf slice, the place where you trip, the place where you lose your focus.

Your shadow issues distort your perspectives on life. You wind up assuming attitudes, judgments, and beliefs that enable your unresolved negative emotions to continue. Shadow issues are all of the places where you fall asleep.

Your mind will tirelessly push your unresolved shadow issues to the surface of your awareness until there are no more to resolve. That is your mind's primal duty. It will never shirk this duty. You can count on this. Your mind will continue performing this duty for your entire life. Because this innate quality is not going away, you may as well accept it and use it for positive gain.

Your shadow issues are as familiar as an old coat, even though they are usually uncomfortable. Actually, most of them are downright painful. But they are so familiar that you are lulled back into them more quietly than a whisper. You so insidiously become the seven-year-old who can't do anything right, the six-year-old who does not fit in. We all have thousands of shadow issues that we have not yet resolved. (At least I have, and everyone I know.)

Once you get stuck in one of your old unconscious loops, you are in a spell. Your rational mind may have gotten stuck on that negative emotion 786 times in the past. You can be stuck in one spell after another, day after day, without ever coming up for air. Unless you take a few cleansing breaths to break the spell, you remain stuck!

Many of your shadow issues came down your family line. They are part of the culture into which you were born. To build your integrity, assume the buck stops with you. You can break the age-old patterns. You heal them one at a time. As an added bonus, as you are breaking your old patterns, your effort helps others around you to break theirs.

Without a discipline to extricate you from one of these spells, you are seldom aware that you have slipped into an unconscious state. The spells are as subtle as falling asleep.

CHAPTER 6

Abdominal Breathing Promotes Self-Esteem

When you develop a habit of breathing out abdominally, it helps you to more quickly notice when your breathing has become shallow or erratic. Then, two or three cleansing breaths snap you awake. When you awaken, the memory of the spell still lingers in your consciousness. Breathing properly gives you awareness of the way external situations have always affected you.

You begin to notice the way certain individuals or situations affect your feelings about yourself. Awareness of how you breathe lets you observe the subtle patterns of your life. That awareness gives you power over situations that used to control you.

You notice the subtle ways you give your power away. You are more keenly aware of when you trample on someone else's toes. Each time you awaken from a spell, you gain new tools and new awareness.

If you take on abdominal breathing as a discipline, you will probably catch yourself breathing shallowly about twenty times a day. That means you wind up replacing about twenty old dysfunctional programs every day. For the first couple of years as you practice this, your self-esteem easily doubles. It continues to grow dramatically every year.

Your self-esteem is like the reflection on the surface of a pond. The calmness or turbulence on the pond's surface is a reflection of your inner state of mind while you are encountering external situations. Each time you awaken, you eliminate one more neurotic response. You replace it with a more functional response that you create from an awakened state. The surface of your lake calms. You plumb greater depths of your awareness.

You grow your self-esteem. Each scene you handle as an aware being builds a new default program. Then, the next time you feel that way, you have an aware program that will handle the feeling. As your self-esteem builds, so does your self-image. You naturally develop greater personal power. With each success you spend more time being aware. Your mind chatter ceases.

Breathe out abdominally for a while, and more of your spirit's unlimited options open up for you. Every moment that you are aware builds a healthier sense of self. You begin to dream and think and build beyond the limits of your past history. You are not your history. What you have done in the past pales in significance to who you are in this moment.

You need not concern yourself about how many times a day you start breathing shallowly and fall asleep. Everyone does that. What is important is how many times you wake up. Take some cleansing breaths and start breathing out from your lower abdomen. What is important is waking up and spending more time awake.

Breath is the first gate to heaven on earth.

Your First Feeling

Have you ever walked into a room and immediately felt uncomfortable? When you walk into an emotionally charged situation, or a person says something or acts in such a way that negates you or disturbs you, there is an immediate reaction that goes on in your body. That reaction is your first feeling. It lasts for only a second or two. In the next moment it is completely gone. If you are not paying attention, you miss it. When you do not pause and feel your first feeling, you go unconscious. After that you are just reacting.

You can go from one unconscious scene to the next without being aware of how you personally feel about what just happened. It is so easy to be distracted by the scene that is going on outside of your body. It takes discipline to make yourself aware of your body's first feeling. And, it takes discipline to pause, then feel that feeling. Pausing to feel your first feeling is the next great frontier. Learning to pay attention to your first feeling is the fifth habit that will change your life. Beyond your feelings there are three more incredible dimensions to plumb.

CHAPTER 7

Learning About Breathing

As I was beginning my adventure into abdominal breathing, I was a medic in the army. Our small medical detachment played a baseball game against a team made up from the 5,000-man artillery battalion. We only had thirty guys to draw from. I did not expect much from our team, but I was pleasantly surprised.

Our first guy up to bat had a stooped-over posture. He was tall and skinny with coke-bottle glasses held together in several places with white tape. He had a pencil holder in his shirt pocket full of pencils and pens. When he moved, his joints articulated as if they were not actually friends. He was definitely not a jock. We all knew he would strike out.

The pitcher for the artillery had an inordinately long wind-up before his pitch. As soon as he began his long wind-up, our batter completely stopped breathing. When the pitcher finally threw the ball, our batter's swing was uncertain. He missed the ball by a mile. Then he had to take a whole bunch of rapid breaths to make up for not breathing at all during the wind-up. It was painful to watch. Two swings later, he was out.

Our next guy up to bat was a tall, lean muscular man who moved with a physical authority that came from years of dominating the hoops. He was a basketball star before the army got him. He exuded an aura of confidence. He hit the bag with his bat a few times and used his bat to point where the ball was going.

He took a couple practice swings, breathing out forcefully with each swing. As the pitcher took his long wind-up, our batter did a series of rapid change-ups in his breathing pattern to stay in synch with the pitcher. As the pitcher threw the ball, our batter breathed out forcefully in perfect timing with his swing. It was a thing of beauty. He uncoiled in a fluid movement that began at his core (one-point center). He hit the ball at the midpoint of his uncoiling and followed all the way through. He crushed the ball.

The ball did not seem to have an arc until it was long past the outfield fence. It took a good fifteen minutes for the other team to find the ball. It went way down into a gully.

During the time the outfielders searched for the ball, I reflected on those two diametrically opposed breathing styles. Each was radically different, and yet each style perfectly matched the individual.

The shallow breather was timid, uncertain of himself. The deep abdominal breather exuded confidence. I started noticing how much breathing affects every aspect of a person's life. That was the day I fully committed to breathing abdominally.

When you see two styles so fundamentally opposite to each other, your mind can fill in the thousands of examples in between. Everywhere I went, I noticed how people breathed. It was so obvious how their breathing affected their lives.

Breathe, Then Act

Healthy, confident people take big abdominal breaths. They really breathe. When something startles them, their first reaction is to take big breaths. Forcefully breathing in and out effectively interrupts the unconscious pattern. They take in a big breath. Then they act.

Neurotic, fearful people, on the other hand, tend to take shallow, erratic breaths. When startled, they stop breathing. They hold their breath. When they start breathing again, they are breathing very shallowly. That ushers in a fearful state of mind for anyone.

Check it out for yourself. Breathe shallowly for a few minutes. Then try to plan out something you definitely want. Courage and confidence, which must have big breaths to sustain, evaporate. Lack and doubt creep into the forefront of your mind after breathing inadequately for a short while.

I became mindful of checking in on my breath. Each time I noticed that I was breathing shallowly, I had usually been doing so for a while. Then I took a few cleansing breaths. The cleansing breaths snapped me right out of the spell every time. Before I learned about abdominal breathing, I tended to get stuck in some unconscious spell at least a dozen times a day. I was usually stuck there for a long while.

With this new discipline, frustration, boredom, depression, or anxieties that would normally darken my mood for hours cleared within two or three cleansing breaths. Big emotions like anger or a major fear took more cleansing breaths to get past.

I began walking around, breathing out forcefully from my lower abdomen. When you are abdominally breathing, you have a body-centered awareness. You move with the full body alertness of a cat. Mental chatter falls away. You are present in this moment.

CHAPTER 8

Life in the Unconscious State

Your rational mind is like an extremely efficient disc jockey. It can handle whatever situation you find yourself in by simply picking the appropriate response for it and playing it.

The mind's response comes from its vast library of all of the physical, mental, and emotional choices you have ever made. Your rational mind's efficiency at instantly choosing and playing just the right tape for the situation at hand is phenomenal. You can instantaneously transition from one task to another, which gives you incredible multitasking skills. The moment you start to do something, that program loads. In an emergency your reaction time can be instantaneous.

Just Doing It

But this ability does have a downside. You do not have to be conscious to function moderately well in literally everything you do. From a spiritual perspective, simply reacting to external events in your environment is sleepwalking. You are not really aware. You are just reacting to external situations.

When you are only reacting to your environment, you tend to be happy in the good times and unhappy in the bad. If there is nothing to do, you tend to be bored. You can spend a lot of time fantasizing about some probable future or immersed in emotional states like frustration, worry, anxiety, anger, or some past/future construction. Basically, you are just going with the flow.

Your mind stays busy reacting to one situation after another with its vast library of rationalizations and dramas. Your mind is always solving problems. If there are no problems to solve, it constructs a problem. When it is in charge, it is never idle.

When someone calls you on the phone, your rational mind instantly puts in the tape, "How to Talk to _____." Each tape is impeccably updated to include all the stuff you had previously discussed, even the stuff you had only considered talking about. The old tapes appear so relevant that you can go through days, weeks, or entire months without having a single original thought. Your mind just runs old tapes that react to what is happening.

You have tapes for everything you have ever done and for all the people with whom you have ever dealt. Your mind has hundreds of thousands of these incredible programs. And it never gets rid of them.

If you have not ridden a bicycle for the last twenty years and you get on a bike today, within seconds riding a bike loads back into your consciousness. Very quickly the cobwebs start to blow out of the old unused program, and you are riding the bike.

These programs are so efficient that it is quite easy to sleepwalk through large segments of time. I believe that throughout history, barely one percent of the general population has been spiritually aware most of the time. More people are awakening every day, although the vast majority still slumber onward.

Most people just do things. They just react. They are not aware of driving their car; they just drive it. Functionally, they are "human doings" instead of human beings. Anytime you are not aware of observing yourself doing something, your rational mind takes control and plays disc jockey with your life.

CHAPTER 9

Running Old Tapes

The tapes your rational mind so seamlessly inserts for all of the things you do are what I call "running old tapes." I gave them that name because your mind always plays just the right program. It plays the one that appears to be the most physically, mentally, and emotionally relevant to whatever situation you find yourself in.

Your body uses old tapes for efficiency. Once you learn to drive a car, ride a bike, or establish any of the hundreds of thousands of skills you have learned, your body maintains continually updated tapes for that skill.

Once established, those skills are available to your entire body and mind the moment you begin to perform them. The program lets you instantly start, right where you left off. You do not have to start from scratch every time.

From then on you never have to go through elaborate checklists prior to performing a complex task you have previously done. As soon as you begin to do something you have done before, the established program automatically loads into the forefront of your mind. Each one of your metaphoric programs includes all the physical skills you have developed to perform that function. Each program also includes the mental skills necessary not only to do the job, but also to handle the diverse problems that come up. That quality alone is incredible. The program includes relevant emotional considerations. Even the attitudes and beliefs integral to performing that particular function load with it.

All of your old tapes are accessible at the speed of thought. That's fast—and highly efficient. Your rational mind can easily load several hundred different programs (or more) in a single hour during a particularly busy time. It is amazing how much multitasking a mother with several young children (and a husband) can perform leading up to breakfast on a school day. Compared to your mind, the most advanced supercomputers in the world are as slow as molasses—and as dumb.

Imagine how long it would take if you had to stop before each complex function you perform and take five or ten seconds to load the thorough checklist required before you were competent to perform the task. The simplest of these programs your mind utilizes would take a fast computer many seconds to load the many thousands of millions of mathematical computations required before it was competent to begin.

The Android and the Human

To really appreciate how amazing your body is, imagine you were part of a large team of highly competent scientists and technicians that was designing and programming an android to perform any one of your normal functions. To make an android simply stand up and walk autonomously has required many years and millions of mathematical computations. That is just to walk. To program mental instructions will require about the same number of mathematical computations—per task. To program the feedback and redundant systems needed for the android to think about what it is doing while planning upcoming tasks will be mind-boggling.

If you were brash enough to think you could program your android out to the emotional level, you would need to add all of the physical and mental requirements together and then multiply that by many thousands of computations—per task.

To program your android to the attitudinal level of performance would require a further quantum increase of memory, computations, and redundant systems. And the android would not be near as smooth at anything as a nine-month old child attempting to feed himself oatmeal.

Now, imagine getting your android to multitask the simplest of functions you perform on any given day. Then you get an inkling of just how impressive these programs really are.

Your mind is competent at performing all of your everyday functions whether you have a single moment of awareness or not. Most people go for long periods of time just reacting to all the complexities of their environment. That is how efficient your mind's programs are. You can do everything you do to a moderate level of efficiency.

Have you ever been driving your car, completely lost in thought, and suddenly realized you have no clue where you are? Nothing seems familiar. You are not aware of how far you have driven. You are unsure whether you have gone past your turnoff.

Had a police officer been driving right behind you, he or she would have observed that you stayed in your lane. You sped up and slowed down with the flow of traffic and generally drove with moderate levels of competency. You handled all those complex driving interactions the whole time that you were unconsciously lost in thought.

Drifting in the Unconscious Current

You could define the above scenario as unconsciousness within unconsciousness, a dream within a dream. Even under those conditions, your mind's program for driving the car can automatically manage your driving with the efficiency of a person talking on a cell phone.

Every time you get in your car to drive, you do not have to think, "Left foot on the clutch, right foot on the gas; hands at ten o'clock and two o'clock; look all around before you back up . . ." You do not need to go over the long checklist a reasonable person needs to know to drive competently. Your driving skills are most likely programmed quite efficiently. (I have seen some evidence to the contrary, though.)

Using your programs, you can cruise through life with minimal awareness and still get by. Most people do. The more undisciplined you are, the greater the amount of time your rational mind will be at the helm, acting like a disc jockey, the absolute master of appropriateness.

However, your rational mind has no awareness of spiritual needs, nor does it ponder any situation you are in relative to soul growth. That is not its job. It just sticks in the tape that matches your situation. Your mind takes care of whatever is happening within the realm of your ethics, tastes, fears, or previous criterions your actions have established. You blithely go with the flow.

Your life will not change much as long as your rational mind is in charge. The only way your mind can evolve is by matching a positive resonance with people around you. If there is spiritual evolution occurring in your environment, your mind will grow along at the trailing edge of the culture in which you are immersed. That is about the only spiritual change your thinking brain is capable of.

Politicians, the media, and advertising people are quite aware of just how unconscious the general public is. Unconsciousness is easy to exploit. Advertising people take direct aim at the population's subconscious minds with jingles and add layouts. They use metaphors that anchor your mind into rationalizing that you can be like that if you use the product that a beautiful or successful person uses. They use the colors, words, and tones (all metaphors) that influence the emotional receptors, and they work. They work because the vast majority of the population remains unconscious.

CHAPTER 10

Advanced Abdominal Breathing

Begin by forcefully breathing out with your lower abdominal muscles as you normally would. On the in breath, you just relax. When you relax your abdominal muscles after forcefully breathing out, your diaphragm muscles involuntarily tighten to pull the floor of your lungs down like a bowl.

You want to feel as if the base of your skull is pushing upward. Relax your shoulders and rock your forehead forward. If you had a miner's lamp on your forehead it would be shining on the ground about forty-five feet in front of you.

Once your posture is anatomically correct, your lung capacity increases. Your lungs have the capacity to take in significantly more oxygen. Now you are ready for advanced breathing.

Taking in Ten Percent More Air

Begin by breathing out forcefully. As your lower abdomen relaxes outward (and you are breathing in), allow the top of your chest to expand. As the top of your chest expands, it naturally lifts upward, pulling in about ten percent more oxygen.

This is the advanced version of abdominal breathing. It cannot happen if the back of your skull is not pushing upward. You must have good posture.

Ten percent more oxygen may not sound like much, but it feels like twice the power, especially when you are playing hard, or if you are facing an important or potentially intimidating situation. Then you have the power.

About 1980 I was looking at Toyota Celicas. They had fuel-injected and non-fuel-injected models, so I test drove both. Compared to the fuel-injected model, the non-fuel injected model felt like it had half as much horsepower.

I said that to the salesman. He remarked that the fuel-injected model only had from seven percent to ten percent more horsepower, depending on how high the engine was revving. Frankly, I found it difficult to believe that the difference was only ten percent at the highest rpm.

After he said that, I wanted to test-drive the fuel-injected model again. When I did I observed that they both had just about the same power at the lower rpms. When the car got up to about 3,500 rpms, the fuel-injected model felt twice as powerful. If you are taking off fast, you are definitely staying above 3,500 rpms.

From that instance, I began to understand how breathing in ten percent more oxygen feels twice as powerful when you are playing hard, working hard, or facing intense mental challenges. When your performance is ten percent better than your best at peak levels, you feel awesome. Ten percent more athletic prowess or ten percent more stamina and clarity in your thinking is a huge increase. While you are breathing deeply, you can focus your attention like a laser. You have the power. When you have the power, confidence follows right along with it.

Breathing in Sports

When a friend and I were barely intermediate skiers, we ventured out onto the west face of KT22 at Squaw Valley. The slope was frighteningly steep at the top. It was not groomed. The snow was deep. With each intense fifty yards, the slope became steeper than it was above. There was a visceral perception that we were dropping into a great maw.

We were way past where we could turn back and clearly out of our depth. We were both commenting about the fine mess we had gotten ourselves into when we heard another skier coming down from above. Actually, we heard great whooshing sounds. It took a moment to figure out what the sounds were.

Long before we heard the clicking of his equipment we heard him breathing huge, determined breaths. He was breathing powerfully and dropping about fifteen yards with each turn, his head facing almost straight down the steep slope, his skis carving out on either side. Twenty or thirty seconds after he blew past us, we saw him ski out at the bottom of the hill and up to the lift nearly a half mile away. Wow!

Considering how deep and irregular the snow was, how unbelievably steep it was, we were in awe. We were also more than a little awestruck at the difficulty we were in. We took more than twenty white-knuckled minutes to descend the remaining 1,500 vertical feet.

That scene branded into my mind. It takes so much oxygen to do what that guy did. It takes a huge amount of skill, too—but you have to take big breaths to ski at his intensity at that altitude.

Most expert skiers have to stop more than a few times and breathe heavily to recover before they can go some more on a run that steep. But most skiers are still breathing the amount of air they breathe at lower elevations. They are not breathing like they are heavily exerting themselves in the rarefied air at the top of a mountain.

When you first get up on a mountain, you are used to breathing at lower elevations. Most of us live down at lower elevations where we are used to breathing less intensely. Up there, the air is a lot thinner. There is a lot less oxygen content at the top of the mountain.

If you breathe as if you are closer to sea level, you will have to stop at short distances and play catch-up with your breath. Breathing like that seriously detracts from having fun. When skiing at the top of a mountain, you have to take as full an abdominal breath as you possibly can, as quickly as you can, to play at expert levels. Then skiing is a lot more fun.

When I was forty years old, I was skiing on a Thursday at Sugar Bowl. There were few skiers on the mountain. I rode up one lift with a young guy. Our skills were about equal, and we hit it off. We wound up skiing together for the rest of the day. Toward the end of the day, we would get to the top of the last mogul field, and I would have to stop to catch my breath while he kept going.

When I caught up with him at the lift, I remarked about his stamina. He said, "Do your legs burn?" I said they did. He said, "That's good. That means you are conditioning your legs." Then he asked if my legs seize up all around. I said they did. He said. "That's bad. That means you are breathing too shallowly."

I had focused on breathing abdominally for twelve years by that time. That day I became more serious about breathing big in sports, really making it an issue—noticing how intensely I have to breathe to play hard. Learning how to breathe adequately allows me to ski just about any run from the top to the bottom without having to stop.

When you are not conditioned, breath is the biggest factor in performance. Breathing in as much air as possible and as deeply as possible fuels your nerves and muscles. Oxygen. You have got to have it if you want to play hard. Breathing correctly gives you the tools to move beyond what used to be your upper limits. Every part of you is excited when you have the energy to play and keep up. When you are excited, you cannot wait to get at it.

Otters of the Universe

If you are not a natural athlete, you have to think about breathing. Most of us are not. The way you should breathe in sports or during a big mental challenge is not the way you breathe when you are just walking around. You have to focus your awareness on breathing big. You have to think about breathing, or you may have difficulty keeping up with the others. The action is less fun. You look for reasons to quit.

We are the otters of the universe. When our actions are no longer fun or we feel like we cannot keep up, we quit doing what we used to have fun doing. That is pretty universal no matter where you go. That is probably why so many older people give up doing the things that used to give them such pleasure. There may be legitimate excuses, like fear of injuries, but the humiliation of not being able to keep up is a huge issue for most people.

When you cannot keep up, you start looking for excuses to quit that activity. Most people progressively give up more of their life each year until the world they create is not fun any more. Then they die. That is definitely not the way I want to create my world. How about you?

When you take full abdominal breaths, it is easy to imagine yourself getting over that hill, dealing with that difficult person, having that fun adventure, facing that fear. Breathe big—live big. The less acceptable alternative is to breathe small—live small.

When you get scared, you start breathing shallowly. That is a normal reaction. Start forcefully breathing out from your lower abdomen, and you may find that what intimidated you may well be within your natural abilities.

CHAPTER 11

Staying Asleep

Throughout history, the vast majority of people have been in-the-moment aware for about two or three years total out of their entire lifetimes. Ironically, people tend to be more aware during times of crisis. People who were not aware during a crisis tended not to live long enough to become ancestors. When a crisis is past, though, it is so easy to allow your rational mind to react to what is going on in the environment. It is so easy to drift along with the flow.

Your mind spins out a continuous series of dramas and rationalizations. There is little attention focused on inner values. Not much changes from year to year. Lack of awareness is the principle reason civilization has evolved at a snail's pace.

In the unconscious state, most people focus on objects or realities external to themselves, what they are reacting to. The mind spins out a constant monologue about lack of money, lack of time, or lack of love. If you have money, the monologue can be about how to protect it, invest it, or make more.

Some of the objects your mind focuses upon are thoughts about what you do not like. The thought forms can be personal, religious, or political. They can range from wondering what people are thinking about you, to making judgments about them. You might be thinking, "If he/she does that, I am going to do this." Or, "Can I get away with not doing this?" The constant mental chatter gives your rational mind purpose—and control.

A large portion of the thought forms concern things your mind is busy protesting. "That should not exist," or, "I am upset about_____."

In the unconscious state, you must learn your lessons a great number of times before you actually commit to change. Your rational mind is busy rationalizing. It produces a lot of drama protesting the lessons. Unsupervised, your rational mind spins out a fairly steady stream of drama aimed at justifying the rationalizations that it is indulging, by thinking about the feelings, instead of feeling them.

Your spirit and soul bring you all of your lessons. Each lesson takes you to your next level of consciousness. The problem is that your mind interprets these lessons as limitations that it should not have to endure. There is an unconscious urge to associate with others who enable you to indulge your unconscious behavior patterns.

The commitment to walking the talk and living the truth gets renegotiated at the slightest test of a person's mettle. The unconscious state is the environment in which fear-based technological advancements historically out-performed socially responsible technology. President Eisenhower, in his final "Iron Cross" speech, said that for the cost of one Trident submarine we can build 500 brick high schools and staff them forever. For the cost of the Iraq war, which had something to do with dwindling oil reserves, we could have developed all of the technology needed to become completely energy independent, employing many millions of people in the process.

When people act unconciously, ethics are the first casualties when money or way of life appear threatened. It has only been during the last half-century that socially responsible technologies have started making gains on society's military/industrial accomplishments. Societal gains exactly parallel the number of individuals who are awakening. In the three and one-half year period between 1964 and 1967, fifty-one million people had a value change and became directed more to their inner values. Becoming inner-directed is the first step in spiritual awakening.

Up to now, the mass consciousness of society has made most decisions based on fears about what *might* happen in the future. Fear-based reactions of society and government evolve into laws. Those very same laws and actions that protect us from others become the stumbling blocks that make it difficult for us to proceed with our magnificent dreams and creative plans.

Fear-based actions are by their nature exclusionary. They exclude someone from doing something. Fear-based societies make up layer upon layer of rules and laws to insulate themselves from others. All of those rules and actions create the obstacle course we must negotiate before we can do what we want. The lion's share of the money we must earn, and the hoops we must jump through just to make a living, result from the rules and actions that are supposed to protect us from others.

For the most part, fear-based concepts do not contribute to your good. They exclude. Exclusion, exclusion, exclusion. Every day that we operate out of fear and guilt, we make more exclusionary rules and actions. They are why you and I have to work so hard to make a living.

I estimate that at least 70 percent of your income is diverted into non-productive, exclusionary actions. For instance, insurance companies that use their talents figuring out ways to deny legitimate care soak up 35 percent of America's health care dollars. We spend something like 85 percent of our health care dollars in the last year of life trying to postpone death. Most of our medical dollars are devoted to prohibitively expensive technologies that fight against disease, instead of a sane and economically viable goal of promoting health.

We spend untold billions of dollars every year building better weapons of destruction to fight our "enemies" when we could partner with them for a fraction of the money. Partnering with them will be an investment that will pay dividends for all of us. Meanwhile, we are investing progressively less money toward educating all of our citizens. When you think about it, there is nothing as ignorant or expensive as war.

It would take only half of what we spend on defensive actions to fix all of the problems we currently face. When enough people wake up, we will demand better.

CHAPTER 12

Awakening

There is nothing that exists that should not be. What is, is. Each time you protest what is, your rational mind takes the helm of your life, takes you out of the moment, and slams you right back into the world of time. There you are, back in the world of pain and suffering.

Acting in an exclusionary manner is very much like rowing out against the incoming tide—or spitting against the wind. You can row for an hour as hard as you possibly can and only gain a hundred yards or so. Exclusionary policies expend an awful lot of energy and have very little gain to show for the efforts.

Inclusive vs. Exclusive

We live in an inclusive universe. *Allow what is.* Allowing what is to exist, without protesting it, is one of the few absolute laws.

All the universe's operating systems are inclusive. All of our physical laws from physics, chemistry, astronomy, and laws that determine how you attract friends, health, intelligence, abundance, or goodness into your life—they are all based upon inclusion.

As more people awaken, more inclusive trails and roads are blazed around and through the fear-based obstacle course society continues to create unconsciously.[1]

---

1 "Do not go where the path may lead; go instead where there is no path and leave a trail." (Ralph Waldo Emerson)

When you make choices based on inclusion, it is like rowing out with the tide. You hardly have to row at all to get where you are going. The wind is at your back. You are in harmony with the natural laws of the universe. What you love loves you back. What you seek seeks you. Love draws you into ever more loving situations. As you learn to awaken sooner and stay awake longer, your realities will naturally become more inclusive.

Life gets easier when you train yourself to focus mainly on what you love. As more people awaken, they tend to create more inclusive programs and situations. We need more of these situations. They give newly awakening people vessels into which they can pour their energies. The better it goes, the better it gets.

What you are feeling this moment folds over on itself and reappears as what is coming at you in the next moment. It is like time looping back on itself. Worry or fear creates more to fear or worry about as time layers back into the next moment.

Based on the law of attraction, focusing on what you love gently moves you further and further away from what you do not desire.[2] Your life is always going in one direction or the other. Because change is a constant in the universe, allow change to move you in the direction of what you love.

Gratitude and appreciation create more to appreciate and be grateful for. When you love others, they tend to love you back. Hold anger toward someone, and he or she is forced to think angry thoughts back at you. You get to choose. You create your own world. Then you live in it.

2   "The Law of Attraction," explained by Abraham, channeled by Esther Hicks.

All Prayers Are Answered

About 2,500 years ago, the Buddha realized that the past and the future are the realm of all pain and suffering. He also said that being stuck in a past/future orientation was the cause of all unsatisfactory experiences. When his followers asked if he was a very high being who incarnated, he said, "No, I am just awake."

In an awakened state, there is no story about this moment. This moment simply and profoundly *is*. Whether you recognize it or not, this moment is the perfect answer to all your prayers and desires. Therefore, allow what is.

The great mystery is how this moment answers everyone's desires and prayers. Einstein, frustrated by not finding a unified theory to link quantum physics to atomic physics, said, "God does not play dice with the universe." By now I imagine he has had enough time on the other side of the veil to check out the situation. I bet he has changed his mind. God does play dice with the universe.

The whole universe is interconnected. It is like an interactive computer game. It gives everyone exactly what he or she expects. Through a sense of order (that appears as chaos, or chance), everyone's prayers and desires are manifested. The answers show up as this moment. The mechanism is a mystery, but you can observe it happening.

We are not taught to think in straight lines. We desire something and in the same breath come up with multiple reasons why we can't have it. We desire something with our thoughts while our negative feelings push it away. The undisciplined way people think makes the answer to their prayers and desires so unrecognizable.

If you could go up to a much higher plane of reality and see all your desires weighed out on scales against all your fears, you would realize that what you have manifested up to this moment is the sum total of your fears and desires. Time just keeps piling them up. Frustrating, isn't it?

Changing Old Thought Patterns

For a lot of people, family holidays can be pressure cookers that stress individuals into acting out painful old patterns. You are fine until the exact moment when someone negates you or pushes one of your hot buttons. Then if you do not pause and feel that first feeling, your breath stops and then goes shallow.

The onset of shallow breathing triggers your rational mind to dig up the past and reactivate your old wounds. You find yourself reacting in the painful way of being that often happens when you are around the family. You can get suckered into painful but so familiar patterns around your family.

Such situations are great times to practice breathing out from your abdomen and feeling those first feelings. You need to be particularly aware of breathing abdominally in situations where you have a history of painful encounters. When you fail to stop and feel that first feeling, you start breathing shallowly. In the next instant, your rational mind loads an old dysfunctional program and you react from that emotional age.

The focus required to breathe out from your lower abdomen may seem daunting at first. But a lifetime of drama, and the pain and suffering from which your rational mind is incapable of extricating itself, is far worse. No matter where you go, there you are.

Breathing out abdominally gives you the prowess to interact with all the skills you have worked so hard to possess. Instead of falling into your old dysfunctional loops and being part of the problem, your rock-solid awareness liberates you and others out of dysfunction.

As you become aware of breathing abdominally, you start noticing more quickly when your breathing goes shallow. When you walk naively into a situation where there are hidden agendas, your breathing instantly takes a direct hit. If you do not pause—and feel that feeling, you are probably not aware that you are reverting to shallow breathing. You get suckered into the dysfunction.

On a positive note, when you walk into a room where everyone is fully conscious, loving, and not running any hidden agendas, your whole being comes up a notch. You all feel safe to speak your truth. Creativity is enhanced. Your mind and feelings soar. You feel wonderfully alive. You are safe and loved. And your breathing comes up a notch.

Association is more powerful than discipline.[3]

3 Paramahansa Yogananda. *Autobiography of a Yogi.* (Self-Realization Fellowship, 1979.)

CHAPTER 13

The Flicker Frequency

Your rational mind has a definite speed limit. It is called the "flicker frequency," which is twenty-four frames per second. The movie industry sets its cameras to the flicker frequency so the film matches the speed at which your mind observes. In the old B westerns, the wagon wheels used to appear to turn backward because the cameras were not tuned to the exact flicker frequency.

Your rational mind's primal function is prediction.[1] It maintains and continuously updates an enormous library of everything it has ever seen, felt, heard, smelled, thought about, or done. At twenty-four frames per second, it compares the similarities of what it is observing to differences recalled from its vast library. Even slight differences are discernable and may raise alarms. That way it can predict the future, based upon the past.

Now that is a concept to read again and ponder. Your rational mind brings all its considerable computing power to every single thing it observes or does. Even watching a basketball bounce across a gymnasium floor, your mind plots the anticipated trajectory of each bounce at twenty-four frames per second. Your mind knows the laws of physics by observation (whether or not you have ever taken a course in the subject). If the ball suddenly bounced in a direction or magnitude that was not predictable, your mind would say, "Whoa! That's not right."

No matter what you are doing or observing, your mind brings all its computing power to play. The amount of computing power your mind commits to every single thing it does or observes is amazing. Most people just use their minds without any awareness of how totally incredible and unique its observations and calculations are.

---

1 Hawkins, Jeff, and Sandra Blakeslee. *On Intelligence.* (Holt Paperbacks, 2005.) A book about harnessing the mind's ability to access its vast library of observations to predict the future. Hawkins proposes that we use this predictive quality to build intelligent robotic machines.

All the whiz-bang calculations your rational mind performs all of the time are its attempts to predict the future based upon the past. If not directed by your spirit, your mind will commit none of its awareness to the present moment. Zero!

Your mind takes you past the present moment like a blur when recalling a past memory or going back to the future. Your mind has no intention of just hanging out in the present. Actually, the rational mind is more than a little intimidated by the now. There is nothing it can control in the present moment. How do you predict the infinity of this moment? If left in charge, your mind quickly goes back to the past or future where it has rules—where it can rationalize what is happening in the world of time.

Your mind is a wonderful servant (in fact it is fabulous), but it is a terrible master. Without direction from your spirit, it will remain 100 percent past/future oriented. In the past you could have done better, so there is a fair amount of guilt. In the future there are too many factors you cannot control, so the future holds fear.

Using brain-mapping procedures, researchers have determined that the average person thinks approximately 60,000 thoughts each day. If your spirit is not guiding its function, those thoughts are going to be based on the past or the future. With your rational mind in charge, most of the thoughts you think today are the same ones you thought about yesterday. Your thought patterns will change very little from day to day.

When you are in the moment, and feeling gratitude, your mind can relax. You have progressively more moments with hardly any thoughts, and no problems to solve or create. Your spirit lives in a sea of bliss, its natural state. When you accept what is happening here and now, your mind can relax. Long periods of time go by with no need to think. From that relaxed state, the most brilliant way to respond becomes apparent. As your mind relaxes, bliss starts to bubble up within your consciousness like water coming up from a spring.

CHAPTER 14

Mastery

When I studied martial arts, my *sensei* (teacher) in a private moment told me about the first time he had to spar with his 89-year-old master.[1] His master was a five-foot-two Korean. My teacher was six-foot-one and powerfully built. Fighting a little old man went against every instinct.

His master leaped up and stepped lithely through the ropes of a regular boxing ring. None of the ropes showed any evidence that he had stepped through them.

My *sensei* thought, "I can do that." He leaped up, deftly placed his foot, and moved catlike through the ropes. From inside of the ring he looked, back at the ropes. They were all waving up and down.

Then the master wanted my teacher to fight him. My teacher did not want to hurt a little old man, so he pulled his punches. His master said, "You not very fast." Moments later he said, "You not very strong." The match was frustrating.

At lunch one of the other teachers said, "I see on the schedule you fought the master today." My teacher said, "If you call it that." The other teacher belly laughed and said, "You don't ever have to worry about hurting him. I go out there and throw everything I've got at him. The best I can ever do with a punch or kick is brush the edge of his *gee*[2] or the top of his hair. He makes no more movement than is absolutely necessary. He easily deflects all of my blows. And at the end of the match, he is not sweating at all. I, on the other hand, can wring the sweat out of my *gee*. Then he critiques my technique, skill levels, and strength."

---

1 After achieving four different black belts, you are considered a master.

2 Martial arts uniform.

At that time I had focused on abdominal breathing for four years. A few months earlier, I had just begun to learn posture and do the exercises that realign your spine.[3] At that time, the whole process those masters went through seemed far beyond anything I could aspire to.

Intellectually, I could see that those people's lives kept getting better until they were masters, but on a gut level I could not imagine myself approaching anywhere near to mastery in my life. I could not imagine myself achieving any level of mastery. Now I see that mastery begins with such a simple step, and then another.

As you add more disciplines to your life, your prowess continues to build. Focus on abdominal breathing, and your self-esteem can double every year for many years. Every part of your body and mind gets better every year, even if you are not participating zealously. All of your efforts are rewarded tenfold. Every step you take toward disciplining your body is multiplied back to you by at least a factor of ten. So much return for so little effort. When you see how much gain you get from even half-heartedly participating, you get motivated to participate on progressively greater levels. It all starts with baby steps.

The Power of Commitment

A quote attributed to W. H. Murray hung on a wall in my treatment room. I read this quote a dozen times a day for about fourteen years:

> Until one is committed, there is hesitancy, the chance to draw back, always ineffectiveness. Concerning all acts of initiative (and creation), there is one elementary truth, the ignorance of which kills countless ideas and splendid plans: that the moment one definitely commits oneself, then providence moves too.

---

3 *Core Strengthening Exercises.* Video by the author, soon to be available at *johnmayfieldchiropractic.com*

All sorts of things occur to help one that never otherwise would have occurred. A whole stream of events issues from the decision, raising in one's favor all manner of unforeseen incidents and meetings and material assistance, which no man could have dreamed would have come his way. I have come to have a newfound respect for one of Goethe's couplets:

"Whatever you can do, or dream you can, begin it. Boldness has genius, power, and magic in it. Begin it now."

Over the years, as I continued to read this quote, a deep understanding of the underlying principles started forming in my mind. I began to see clearly that commitment is the access code to the universe.

Without commitment, you are stuck. The wheels fall off your car. You just sit there with all possibility and potential surrounding you. You sit there, not moving.

The universe is like an interactive computer game where all of your desires or prayers are answered as you move through the game's maze. When you commit to something, anything, the doors behind you begin to close. The doors in the direction you commit to start blowing open. Then your life is propelled in that direction.

Until you make that commitment, those doors do not open. Without commitment, very little changes in your life. As you become more decisive, especially about little things, you experience significant changes in your life. You progressively fulfill more of your hopes and dreams.

Because you are a spirit, living in a universe with spiritual rules, all manner of unforeseen things occur as the direct result of a commitment. The entire spiritual kingdom conspires to help you. When you commit, your life takes on a trajectory, a direction of movement. This is important because when you arrive at your life's various crossroads, the teacher is there. The mystery is there. The gift is there. In an unconscious state, people tend to be myopic. They fail to notice these three gifts at every crossroad of their lives.

Next time a lesson comes up, accept what is. Then look around. There, just beyond the depth of where you would normally look, is the mystery. The teacher is there, and so is the gift. They are always there at every lesson.

Freedom is the fruit of your self-disciplines. If you want more freedom, be more disciplined. Look around you at people you know who have figured out how to be free. Notice how disciplined they are. At the opposite polarity, be aware of people who have very little discipline in their lives. Notice how life seems to entangle and encumber them every way they turn.

Life is a paradox. The more you try to be free, the more you are encumbered. The more disciplined you become, the more freedom you experience. True freedom is not mysterious. It follows simple laws.

Your spirit's power and magnificence are always pushing you up into higher limits of what you can believe and experience. The more disciplined and decisive you are, the faster you progress and the higher you go in this life.

Your upper limits keep expanding. The more you choose to live in the upper limits of your life, the more magnificent life becomes for you. Age empowers you. I love this understanding. The more disciplined you are, the more age empowers you. You want to look back and say, "Yeah, I did that!"

Awareness is like the headlights of your car shining into the darkness. You can only see for the short distance your headlights illuminate. As you learn to breathe out from your abdomen through more situations, your light and your power shine progressively further into the night of your (yet) undiscovered world.[4] Breathing abdominally is like having super halogen lights.

You are an immortal being who is for a short time incarnated into a physical body, a spirit having a human experience. The entire universe is your playground. When you believe that you are an immortal being of great beauty, your posture and breathing begin to reflect that reality. Life just keeps getting better. This is the way life is meant to be.

4 Power is the ability to do what you say you will do, and do it in a reasonable time period.

CHAPTER 15

The Posture of Awareness

The simple movements you make from one moment to the next can heal you. They can feel magical or slowly destroy you, plunging you ever deeper into a Muggle-like world of drudgery and effort. Time keeps score.

With good posture, time is kind to you. You look better. You feel better. It is all so simple. This is the second habit that will profoundly change your life.

Your posture instructs others how you expect them to respond to you. What does your posture say to others? Good posture is elegant. It garners respect. You are stronger, more flexible. Every cell operates at its fullest potential. You gain more endurance. Simply going for a walk in good posture can eliminate most of the spinal misalignments in your body.

Do you remember how exciting it felt to do simple movements when you were a child? The thrill of deftly avoiding the dodge ball during recess? The joy of feeling you could run like the wind? The first time you rode your bicycle without your father running along beside you? Reflect back to some of the joyous physical experiences you remember as a child.

One of my fondest childhood memories is how exciting my body felt at twilight during the summer. The summertime heat would give way to the magical time of twilight. I remember fearlessly jumping barefoot over my mother's big old thorny pyracantha bush, as light as a feather. It felt like the physical constraints that held me earthbound were loosened, and I could run like the wind.

That magical feeling in your body is how you are supposed to feel. You can recapture the pure joy of movement you experienced as a child. It is not gone forever. Simple, correct posture brings it back. Learning to walk and move correctly brings you back to the childhood joy of pure movement. You come back into the moment. Magic lives in the ever-present moment, and your everyday movements can take you there.

Your body's design is the essence of simplicity. Part of the simplicity is that correct posture has no history of trauma. Walking correctly feels good while it is healing you. With every step you take, you can reprogram a very advanced instrument—your body—back to true. You can heal your self, one step at a time.

Every trauma you accept into your body has affected how you move through life. You take a hard fall off of your bike. The person you love falls in love with your best friend. One by one you collect mental, emotional, and physical traumas into your body. With each trauma you accept into your posture and gait, you lose a little more of your innocence. You lose the magic of walking.

Your traumas take on a life of their own. Your posture and breathing become compromised. You move in such a way that one moment, one movement at a time, you create your complete history of trauma. Your posture unconsciously reflects and re-creates the cumulative traumas you have collected during your life. You find yourself standing and moving that way, and after a while, the traumas just seem to be a part of you. You identify with your traumas and give them names like "my bad knee."

Your injuries insinuate themselves into your belief systems. Your beliefs become compromised. This brings you to a place where you believe that childhood innocence is naive. You have continuously re-created your injuries for so long that they appear to be permanent.

Walking becomes the chore you have to do to get to your destination. So, you park as close as you can wherever you go, and inwardly you begrudge the short distances you have to walk.

Does anything seem wrong with this picture?

CHAPTER 16

Differences Between Dogs and Cats

Once as a teenager I saw a cat get caught up in one of my friend's feet. He was in a big hurry, moving too fast. The cat got slammed hard against a wall. The cat's reaction to the trauma of being kicked into a wall was incredible. He got up, shook it off, and walked away as though he was thinking, "That never happened." No limping, no favoring the trauma. One second later, and the cat had already put the trauma behind him.

Although that incident made a profound impression on me, I did not understand the lesson until many years later. Now I understand that cats live in the moment. They rarely show residual trauma in their bodies after the moment is past. For a cat, the past is past. The third habit that will change your life is to walk away from your injuries like a cat.

The world of cats is a fascinating place. Cats that spend their time outdoors are like psychic kung fu masters. With their consciousness focused laser-like in the now, cats do not linger in self-pity by limping, gimping, or favoring an injury. They do not squander their life force by allowing their attention to dwell on injuries of the past.

Cats heal very fast. Their focus is on reflecting the highest quality of being a cat. Rudyard Kipling's summary still says it best: "I am the cat who walks by himself and all places are alike to me."

Giving Away Power

Dogs are not quite as bad as humans about favoring an injury, but they are far worse than cats. They react more like people when they get hurt. They show it. Most dogs will milk the trauma for all its worth. A dog will limp around for days garnering sympathy for his pain. At least for a while, the trauma becomes part of his gait, an integral part of his movements. Luckily for dogs, their attention span is not as long as ours. They soon forget. After awhile they drop the limp.

When you limp or move into postures of pain avoidance, you create sensory and motor feedback loops. With each ill-repeated movement, the feedback loops remake the painful memory of the past and imprint it onto whatever you currently perceive.

Secondary complications, resulting from favoring injuries, create far worse problems than your original trauma. The limp affects your skeletal frame by creating seemingly permanent misalignment patterns. Organ systems become compromised. In physical situations, reaction times are compromised, making you vulnerable to further trauma. The misalignments make your bones arthritic. Over time your health deteriorates. Favoring injuries is a bad idea on every level.

In the unconscious state, you tend to make subtle shifts in posture or gait to move away from tension, aches, and pains. You shift your weight onto your "good" leg. If your neck hurts, you tend to let your head drop down and forward.

People give their power away in all the ways they slump. A person who is taller than his or her friends may slump down to the friends' height so as not to "tower over them." A young woman lets her shoulders slump forward to draw attention away from her breasts. Slumping can be a protest against parental control or values.

The moment you slump, your rational mind takes control of your perceptions. The transition into unconsciousness is so smooth you rarely notice. Faulty posture causes your rational mind to take control just like shallow breathing does.

Each faulty posture is a vessel that contains vast libraries of pain and suffering. The pain and suffering are stored in your memory as combined sensory and motor feedback loops. Once the feeling takes you back into that particular loop, it activates the thoughts and physical memories attached to it. The feedback loop contains attitudes and beliefs that allow you to justify continuing to feel the way you do in that posture.

When you are caught in one of these feedback loops, your mind has whisked you away from the here and now. You are not really here now. Technically, you are in an artificial construct made up of some past or future projection.

The sensory/motor feedback loop seems "appropriate" to what your eyes are focusing on. You can easily believe that "this" is reality. Your mind has superimposed an artificial past or future construct over what you currently perceive.

Act Like a Cat

When I was a young chiropractor, a Hollywood stunt man retired and moved to my town. He had spent a career falling off horses and buildings, wrecking cars, and doing whatever was too dangerous for the actors to do themselves.

One day I saw him in town and he said, "I have an appointment to see you tomorrow." I said, "Great!" I really liked him and looked forward to seeing him. In the middle of the night, though, I woke up in a sweat, worrying that he might be held together with duct tape and bailing wire.

When he arrived at my office the next day, he carried his most recent X-rays. "Standard procedure," he said as he handed them to me. I put them up on the view box. Remarkably, his spine looked good. Actually, his spine looked a whole lot better than most people his age.

He was in his late sixties, and his spinal column looked like it belonged to a young man. As I was working on him, I could not fathom how he could have had a career in such a traumatic profession and present such a healthy spine.

As I was grappling with the question of how he could spend a lifetime thrashing himself and not show it, he said, "In the industry, when we do a gag"—that is what they call a stunt—"my team sets up every aspect of the stunt carefully in advance. If I am to crash a car into a brick wall, the wall is constructed of bricks that weigh less than one-third of what a normal brick weighs. They are stacked with a light mortar that has no cement in it. As the crew sets up the gag, they try to think of everything.

"But sometimes things go wrong. The car might hit so hard that my rib cage slams into the armrest of the car, and I crack a couple of ribs. I groan for a few labored breaths. Then I remember that there are 300 people on the back-lot tour, watching the gag. I take a few more breaths to get myself together. Then I look up and wave at the crowd. They cheer. As I get out of the car it may take a few steps to get the limp out. Then I walk off to the trailer like 'nothing happened.'

"My crew saw what happened. They were quite aware of how long it took for me to look up and wave. Back at the trailer, they help me take off my shirt and tape up my ribs. Then we do triage to decide whether to take me to the chiropractor, the physical therapist, or the orthopedist. I grab my X-rays out of the filing cabinet, and off we go."

From that conversation I "got" that being a stunt man made him act like a cat. No matter what happened, he always walked away as if the injury never happened. The couple of breaths he took before he looked up and waved at the crowd interrupted him from a pattern of focusing his attention on the injury. The breaths brought him back to his present time awareness: "It was a gag."

Every organ, every function in your entire body depends on correct posture. Because you are mostly energy, you really do not want kinks in all your circulatory systems. If you let one of your feet toe out and your head drop down and forward for only a half an inch, you establish as many as a dozen misalignments in your spine and extremities.

These misalignments kink your energy flow and create seemingly unrelated problems with organ malfunctions and the like. The nerves going to every organ must exit from the sides of your vertebrae. Kink a vertebra with bad posture, and with each step the related organ is in trouble.

Your misalignments are not permanent. They are only temporary—even if you have reproduced them, one step at a time, for years. After awhile, though, the misalignments become such a part of your habit patterns that you come to believe they *are* permanent.

The main reason they seem permanent is because for years you have continued to stand and walk the same way. You re-create your injuries one movement, one step at a time.

Go for a two or three-mile walk with correct posture and you untwist most of the misalignments out of your spinal column and extremities. Walking correctly gets the knots out of your rope. Those pesky symptoms that seemed so permanent turn out to be temporary. Return to bad posture, and they come back. Habits shape your reality. The only thing permanent is change.

In health, every cell in your body communicates clearly with every other cell. That's it. That is dynamic health. Poetry in motion. You dance through life. Every movement is a source of healing. This is how it's supposed to be.

Your feet are parallel. You are breathing out forcefully from your lower abdomen. Your torso and neck are erect. You feel the back of your skull naturally pushing upward. You relax your shoulders. Life is good. You want to keep increasing the repertoire of occasions where you dance through life.

CHAPTER 17

Nonverbal Communication

Most of your communication with others is nonverbal. Posture is the main player in your nonverbal communications.

Your posture is actually a demand. It demands of others around you how you expect to be considered or treated. Everyone responds to your posture, whether they are conscious of it or not.

Elegant posture creates an aura that influences others to treat you with elegance and respect. Walk around with your head dropped down and projecting out there in the future, and people around you tend to think that you mean "later." Of course, you would prefer for it to happen now.

When you see someone who is slumped down, your unconscious reaction is to discount that person. Your reaction occurs long before you have time to think about it. The person's posture obviously does not portray respect for himself or others. How likely would you be to hire someone who slumped down in the chair when you asked pointed questions?

People notice your posture. How you sit and stand, and whether you are paying attention, profoundly affect people's assessments of you. They notice your facial expression, the tone of your voice, and how open your posture is to them. Based on what they observe, they make their decisions (quite often unconsciously) about trusting you, how they will respond to you, and how much of their energy and respect they will commit to you.

When your posture looks good, you feel good. All your circulatory systems are wide open and running. That allows your body's innate intelligence to maintain clear, open communication channels throughout your body.

The clear communication creates a dynamic state of health within your body and mind. Your health shines through. Your self-esteem comes up a notch. Your mind processes thoughts more efficiently. You make better decisions. All your parts work better. People notice.

CHAPTER 18

Bad Posture Holds Pain and Suffering

Every incorrect posture is a primal way of giving your power away. It is how you take yourself down a notch so you do not outshine your peers. We usually begin creating our posture in early childhood. We learn to be more afraid of letting others see our power or beauty than letting them see our faults.

The moment you slump, your rational (unconscious) mind accesses your memories linked to the movement. Each faulty posture has its own library of unresolved thoughts, actions, feelings, and beliefs. Your mind chooses the earliest unresolved memory (or a possible future you have angst about) which that posture holds a charge on. Then it projects that unresolved event over the top of the current moment.

Each faulty posture is a container that holds vast histories of trauma. The faulty postures also contain your fears about the future. Some of the postures, such as letting your head drop down and forward, represent such a universally common way of giving power away that they hold the entire history of your culture's pain and suffering.

The instant you unconsciously slump, your rational mind takes control by putting a spin on whatever you are doing. Your mind reminds you about how hard you have to work, how others are better off than you (or you are than they), how much you lack, incessant desires, and countless other dramas you have heard many times before.

The thoughts, feelings, and attitudes contained within that compromised posture are acted out, not only by you, but also by other people in your immediate environment. When you are unconscious, the past/future constructs your rational mind continuously projects seem so real. For example, if you are projecting the status of being a victim, others around you, who are also unconscious, will play their parts in your drama by taking advantage of you.

Your rational mind uses a number of these unconscious mechanisms to continuously re-create your pain body. Otherwise it begins to fade.

If you walk up a hill leaning forward (slumping), your mind begins spinning its drama. As familiar as your shadow, the past memory or future projection plays across your mind. In response to your leaning-forward posture as you walk, your rational mind instantly projects you into a drama. The drama takes some negative memory you have not resolved and projects it over the top of this particular moment.

The seduction is that the projection is instantaneous and plausible. Within microseconds your mind takes you back to the first moment that particular feeling was left unresolved—and allows you to indulge the unresolved negativity in this moment.

The stories your mind weaves appear so appropriate, so all-encompassing and seductive. These unresolved stories are unpleasant, but they are as familiar as an old coat. You can suspend your disbelief, like you do in a well-constructed movie. For as long as you remain unconscious, you can assume that the artificial construct is real.

It is impossible to stay in the present moment when your head is thrust out in the future. Even when you are doing your best to stay in the present moment, a head-forward posture will be constantly, unconsciously pulling your mind into one of its past or future constructs. In the past or the future, you have no traction. In the illusory world of time, you have no power to manifest your heart's desires.

The only place where you have any power is in the now. Correct posture has no past, no future. There is only now.

Believing Is Seeing

To really get what I am saying, you must understand that your eyes are not merely cameras. In an unconscious state of mind, you do not "see" with your eyes. Because your rational mind unconsciously relates *everything* to the past or future, it spins out a story. The story transports you into a past/future construct that allows you to indulge your unresolved emotions. The dramas your mind weaves have seemed appropriate to what your eyes are focusing on for as long as you can remember.

If not guided by your spirit, your mind will continuously project scenes that "seem" appropriate to what your eyes are focusing on. Your mind gets used to being in control.

What you are seeing, via the computer-like qualities of your rational mind, may have happened many years ago somewhere else. Or, you may be projecting a fantasy future, based on what you fear could happen. You may be projecting something that you are angry about, something that "might" happen. Because what you focus your mind upon manifests into being, "What I fear has come upon me."

Your unconscious mind's projections are never as wonderful as being in "this" moment. But, hey, if you are not aware of observing yourself doing what you are doing, you really are not here.

Imagine, for example, that you are doing the mundane portion of a job and it is fulfilling all your prayers from as far back as you can fathom. The bliss, which your spirit is continually immersed in, is permeating all that you are experiencing. The bliss of your spirit is bubbling up into your conscious awareness like a spring of water. You are having a good time.

Then, for some reason, you unconsciously slump into some old posture. Of course that posture has vast amounts of unconscious memories of "having to work so hard." In the instant that you slump, your rational mind takes control of your perceptions. The transformation is slick. You rarely notice the seduction.

In the old tape you are running, your history of having to work so hard is superimposed over the job that was, only a moment ago, fulfilling all your wishes or prayers. The "spin" projects how unfair it is that other people are having such a good time while you have to work so hard.

When you view your rational mind's projections from the logic of your spirit, they are not appropriate. When you are in the moment, you are in love. You are fulfilled. In the illusory world of time, you live in the realm of pain and suffering. The projections of your rational mind are about controlling the situation, and there is always a tinge of fear and guilt. The projections are not about loving this moment.

Your mind will continue to spin out this story, or others like it, for hours, days, and years if you allow it. Your mind has thousands of such stories to project. Without direction from your spirit, your mind perpetually problem solves. If there is no problem, before long it will create one for you to focus on.

Problem solving and predicting the future, based on the past, are the functions of your rational mind. Do you want to spend the rest of your days focusing on problems and drama?

CHAPTER 19

The World You Create

Take a few cleansing breaths. Resume good posture. I like to do about fifteen spinal twists to immerse myself back in the world I am creating. Instantly (no slower than that) you are back. You are awake. A great habit to develop is to allow what "is" to exist. What is, is.

You cannot change what is, but you can always choose how you respond to it. One of the great Zen masters used to ask his students, "Is there anything in this moment you would change?"

As you return to your natural state, which is bliss, you return to the garden of Eden. Actually, your spirit has never left the garden. The garden of Eden is now. It was now. It will always be now. There is only now.

Heaven and hell exist right here on earth. Each moment you choose to live in heaven or hell. You can slump into that tired old posture, and instantly your rational mind takes over. Pain and suffering are the fruit of the unconscious state. That seems like hell to me.

Your spirit lives in an environment, a sea, of bliss. Bliss is your spirit's natural state. Good posture and abdominal breathing help you to continually return to this moment. Relax into the awakened state, and bliss naturally begins to bubble up like water from a spring.

When you "get" that this moment is the manifestation of all of your wishes and prayers, you can let go of the past and the future. You create your own world, and then you live in it. There is nothing in the future or the past that is even half as wonderful as now. There never was.

You can return to the moment by focusing your awareness on the texture of what you are touching, taking in the warmth of the sun, sensing the wind's caress, or enlivening any of your five senses with whatever you are doing. Focusing your awareness on the simple sensory perceptions of the mundane tasks you are performing brings your focus back to experiencing what is going on now, here and now. This is wakefulness, being aware.

CHAPTER 20

Walking on the Beach

In 1974, my girlfriend and I went on vacation. We stopped in Florence, Oregon, and spent the night in a nice little motel on the beach. I woke up the next morning at first light hurting in about a dozen places from old injuries. At the time I was a few months into learning the Alexander Technique of posture, a method for discovering new ways of sitting, standing, breathing, and moving that put less pressure on your body and allow you to perform daily activities with greater ease and efficiency.

The aches represented pain I had lived with for years. I could not stay in bed a minute longer, so I went for a walk on the beach. I knew my girlfriend would sleep for a few more hours.

After walking for about a mile, I started feeling sorry for myself for all of the pain I constantly experienced. I felt something behind me. I looked back. There was no one on the beach. What was there when I turned around were my tracks in the sand. They drew my full attention. My footprints looked really bad.

I doubled back about a hundred yards to study the tracks I had made before becoming self-conscious. I studied them as if I were tracking another person. Studying my tracks in the third person freed me up to be more objective.

I had recently studied the monograph of a Swiss chiropractor, Dr. Fred Illi, who performed more than twenty thousand motion picture X-ray studies of people walking on a treadmill. This was my first real opportunity to field-test the knowledge.

The guy's right foot turned out about twenty degrees. That is a lot. He landed on the outer part of his heel. Then his heel wobbled inward so it came down flat on the sand.

As he came into the midstance portion of his gait, his foot once again wobbled outward and then came back inward so it would be flat. This caused the sand to spill into both the heel and the midportion of his footprint from both sides.

As he proceeded to the push-off portion of his gait, his right foot twisted laterally (like mashing a cigarette out), obliterating the front two-thirds of every right footprint for as far back down the beach as I could see.

So, his ankle wobbled outward and then back inward a couple of times each step. Then he added a twist-off motion with his right foot at the push-off portion of his gait. With every step, this guy's right knee had to be making a lot of movements a knee is not designed to do. This guy must be having knee problems.

What a coincidence. So was I.

Meanwhile, the footprint of his left foot was completely intact. It was whole. I could have made a clear plaster cast of each one of the left footprints from that sandy beach.

As I wondered why he twisted his right foot laterally, I realized that turning his right foot out shortened the stride of his right leg by at least five-eighths of an inch. If he did not make the twist-off movement with his foot, he would be walking in a big circle to the right. After about two days of supposedly walking in a straight line, this guy could arrive right back where he started. That made me laugh.

After studying those tracks, I decided to walk with both feet parallel. When I had walked for a hundred yards, I stopped and rechecked my footprints. My right foot was still toed out, just not as far. Now it was about seven degrees instead of twenty. Because the right foot was still toed out, it still had the four troublesome wobbles and the nasty obliteration of two-thirds of the footprint. Dang!

I placed my feet parallel to one another while I stood there looking down at them. Then I stood up erect. When I did, my entire right leg felt like it had a steel rod running down the outside of it. My right foot felt pigeon-toed (toed inward) by about seven degrees.

Standing with my feet parallel felt weird. It felt unnatural. But I decided that, no matter how unnatural my right leg felt, I was going to walk down that beach with my feet parallel.

Every hundred yards I rechecked my footprints. Each time, both prints were perfect. I could have lifted a perfect plaster cast of either foot. *Yes!* Then I just walked, enjoying the magnificent sunrise and the sea.

After walking about three miles, I stopped cold in my tracks. All my pains had vanished. Up until that moment, on a one-to-ten pain scale, I had ten areas that hurt constantly at seven or eight. My right knee always ached. For the past ten years, I could predict the weather with uncanny accuracy by where and how much my right knee hurt.

Now all my pains were completely gone. Even the minor symptoms I had lived with for years, like my constant stiff neck, the dull, slight headache that was always there and sometimes went nova, and my constant stomach discomfort. All were totally gone. When you are used to living with a lot of aches and pain constantly, having them all disappear will definitely get your attention.

I had walked the misalignments out of my spine by walking with correct posture. When my spine realigned, all of my symptoms disappeared. That got my complete attention. That moment on the beach was an epiphany.

That was when I experienced, within my own body, the miracle of correct posture. I do not banter the word "miracle" about lightly, either.

Why Keep Your Feet Parallel?

There is a reason why boxers and high-level tennis players do not walk like a duck with their feet splayed outward. With your feet splayed out, you give up too much prowess. You lose a lot of your freedom of movement. Reaction times slow down.

Toeing your feet outward makes your inner leg muscles weak. This forces your outer leg muscles to overdevelop. The ensuing imbalance gives your knees the kind of brittle, inflexible strength that allows them to get hurt.

When you walk and move with both feet parallel (aiming the same direction), your inner and outer leg and pelvis muscles are forced to work with equal strength. Because of that, your inner leg muscles develop and tone up. In every sport or physical activity, your inner leg muscles give you the most physical prowess. As the strength and stamina of these muscles increase, you gain more flexibility and a greater sense of balance.

Check yourself out. Stand up with your feet parallel. Then feel the muscle tonus of your inner thigh muscles compared to your outer thigh muscles. Are your inner muscles as toned up as your outer muscles? If not, you definitely stand or walk with your feet toed out. Muscles have the same tendencies people have. Your muscles will be as lazy as you allow.

If you allow one or both feet to toe out, your hip, knee, and ankle joints take a beating with every step. Most people think this kind of deterioration is "old age." It is definitely not old age. Age is meant to empower you.

Walking in good posture with your feet parallel progressively heals those same joints by a process of joint remodeling. This process occurs at the cellular level, where all your muscle, ligament, and bone cells are continuously replaced. The marriage of form (your musculoskeletal system) and function (correct posture) is a dynamic, ever-changing process. With bad posture the results are, well—bad.

In the dance between form and function, good posture constantly models your bones toward a more efficient shape. Postures that let gravity punch you down cause your bones to break down and deteriorate into arthritic spurring, bones flattening out, degenerative discs, and a host of other less-than-glamorous changes.

The only constant is change. Every cell in your body lives out its life and is completely replaced within a few months. Correct posture and gait provide a template that continually reshapes your form into the most efficient shape possible to handle whatever life activities you are demanding of it.

CHAPTER 21

Posture Begins in *Hara*

In Japanese culture, your "one-point center" is called *hara*. It is the absolute midpoint between your upper body and your lower body. It is your place of power, the ancient heart of your spiritual body.

Hara is two finger-widths below your naval and straight back to the front of your fourth lumbar vertebra, your second-to-the-bottom vertebra. *Hara* is the most important location in your body.

Your movements begin and end in this exact part of your body. Dancers and martial artists move from this point, whether they know it as *hara* or not. You cannot do spin moves or perform complex dance movements (or even maintain good balance) without having your center of gravity at this point. The purpose of all postural considerations can be summarized as *focusing your awareness in* hara.

In Western cultures we do not even have a name for our "one-point center" of awareness. We basically have no dialogue—zero—about where we should focus our consciousness. There is no awareness about this extremely important part of our body. The utter lack of awareness of where our absolute center is has to be the main reason we Westerners lack clear, firm boundaries, why we have so many co-dependant tendencies.

Breathing out forcefully focuses your spirit fully into *hara*. Then your spirit incarnates all the way into your body—all the way down to your fingernails and toenails. Once your spirit is centered in *hara* it can fully energize every part of your body.

Your multi-dimensional body cannot fully contain all the power of your spirit. From your one-point center, the energy from your spirit fills your body to overflowing. As the energy pushes outward through all your subtle energetic centers, it creates fields of energy that trail out behind you like the wake of a giant ship going through the water.

Your Spirit's Energies
Pushing Downward

When your feet are parallel, your legs completely fill up with spiritual power until your spiritual energy is pushing downward from the balls of your feet. In martial arts, the energy centers at the balls of your feet are called "bubbling wells." Running your energy out bubbling wells makes you as rooted as an oak tree. Your balance is more stable. You become a force of nature.

The subtle energy from your spirit that is pushing downward through bubbling wells has a Sherwood green hue. When these energy centers activate, they allow you to experience a more intimate relationship with the elemental kingdom—which includes the spirits of the plants and animals, the rock beings, and the cloud people. Plants and trees have an emotional life as powerful as yours. People who have green thumbs know this directly.

Indigenous people have maintained their communication with the elemental kingdom. It is time for us to reclaim our connection, to come back into the garden. There are exciting inner worlds to discover.

Your Spirit's Energy
Pushing Upward

When you locate your awareness in *hara*, your spirit's energy also push upward, filling your whole torso with energy. As your torso fills, it becomes easier for your trunk to maintain erect posture. Spiritual energy keeps surging upward and pushes your shoulders outward.

As you relax your shoulders, they drop down and forward at the ends. When your shoulders are both full of energy and relaxed, they become a stable flexible platform for your neck and head.

Relaxing your shoulders allows the upward-surging energy of your spirit to completely fill up your neck and head. *The energy continues to exert pressure upward, pushing the back of your skull upward.* Always upward. Rock your forehead forward so that if you had a miner's lamp on your forehead, it would be aiming on the ground forty-five feet in front of you.

Rocking your forehead forward locks in your core spiritual energy (also known as the Indian *kundalini* energy), so it builds up its strength and intensity within your body.

When your head thrusts out forward and you let the back of your skull drop down, your spiritual energy dissipates out the back of your skull, much as heat or cool air flows from a building with all the windows wide open.

Without spiritual energy filling your body, it is limp. It takes too much effort to keep your body erect. When your spirit lives in *hara*, your entire body fills up with energy. It is like blowing up an air mattress. The air holds the mattress erect. *When your body is full of energy, it is easier to maintain an erect posture.* The better it goes, the better it gets.

CHAPTER 22

Living at Your Upper Limits

Make it your goal to have twice as good posture this year as you had last year. Even a half-hearted effort gives back such wonderful rewards that you soon want more. Remember, every effort you make towards your health is rewarded by a factor of ten. For every unit of energy you put toward healing, you are rewarded by ten times as much from your body. That is a one thousand percent return on your investment.

Older people make great studies. Older people who are so alive are younger at heart. They stand and sit erect. They eat more fresh vegetables and fruit. They are more active. They do more fun things. Because they are excited about what they do, their lives are more exciting. Although they may have lived a lot of years, they are not "old."

When you make a habit of maintaining erect posture and gait, you increase your health and vitality every year. Stand more erect. Walk with a healthy gait. You will experience your life force doubling each year for years to come. Age will be kind to you.

Will you commit to having posture twice as good as what you had the year before? If you make this decision, you will not regret it.

Consider a life where you and your loved ones are living progressively into the "upper limits" of your lives. That is where all the fun and goodness are. Every year, life is more exciting. Every year, you have more personal power.

I have personally tried and discarded at least two hundred health disciplines after they proved marginally effective. *The habits in this book are the taproot habits that firmly connect you to the source of your power.* They are the few that never cease helping you live progressively into the upper limits of your life.

The fruit of these habits is a freedom that unfolds progressively more every year into something greater than you ever imagined your life could become.

Every part of your body is transcendent. Each level of health you step up to helps you access the next level of goodness. Each year you gain more mastery. You become the promise of yourself. Your body and your mind are more fulfilled each year. Life is more fun as you grow older. Age empowers you.

CHAPTER 23

Gaining Energy When You Stand or Walk

Your Lower Back's Two Opposing Rules

Rule 1: When you stand or walk on flat ground, tuck your buttocks down and breathe out forcefully from hara. Your belt buckle aims straight toward the horizon. As you breathe out forcefully, it balances the strength and tonus of your abdominal muscles to the strength and tonus of your back muscles. All of the power of your lower body is right there, balanced and accessible to you.

When your belt buckle is aiming at the ground your hips sway out over your toes, causing more problems than you can afford. Because everyone is unique, this posture causes an infinite number of symptoms—all bad. Most people with back problems also have their belt buckles aiming at the ground, their heads forward, and their feet toed out.

Rule 2: For everything other than standing or walking on flat ground, stick your buttocks out backward.

You have to really stick your buttocks out—further than you think—to maintain a healthy low back curve. When your low back curve goes straight, your stress doubles. You are more easily injured. You lose half of the strength of your low back. Most people lift incorrectly, and coincidently most people have low back problems when they have to do a lot of lifting.

Sticking your buttocks out (while keeping your torso erect) allows you to lift something properly without hurting yourself. It lets you sit down or get up from a sitting position elegantly. You walk upstairs or uphill without pathologically bowing your low back out backwards. When you maintain a healthy low back curve, everything you do heals you. Your body and your consciousness keep refining to higher levels of organization.

Try this test. Put your hand on your lower back and see if you can sit down and get back up without blowing the curve out backward. You have to really stick your buttocks out to do this, don't you?

Healing Your Low Back Curve

When you walk up a hill or stairs, keep your upper body and head erect. Stick your buttocks out backward. This posture is quite elegant.

When walking erect on uneven ground, sticking your buttocks out makes you stable. It is like the difference between driving off-road in a 2-wheel drive vehicle or a 4-wheel drive vehicle with big knobby tires.

These two opposing rules actually work together to maintain your lower back's healthy concave (inward) curvature without allowing it to bow out backward or become too swayback. That way you can live powerfully without harming yourself. You can lift much more than you normally could without hurting yourself. Consciously performing your acts of daily living heals your low back and increases your prowess each year. Hard work buffs your muscles.

The big concave cables on a suspension bridge like San Francisco's Golden Gate Bridge give the span 90 percent of its strength. The same goes for your low back (and neck). Keeping a healthy concave curve, no matter what you are doing, is where you get 90 percent of your strength.

Stick your buttocks out, and walk erect up the stairs. This posture is as efficient as it is elegant. If you see another person walk up hills or stairs in this manner, you will see how vibrant, powerful, and elegant it looks.

When you arrive at the top of the stairs or the hill, you have toned up all of your muscles equally. The exertion has brought you to a state of balanced power. The front and back muscles of your neck, torso, pelvis, and legs are equally toned. You are ready for anything. The movements you perform every day contribute to your healing.

In the beginning, climbing stairs or hills this way uses different muscles than you are accustomed to using. Using new muscles can cause you to feel more tired until your body gets used to it. Anything you do not normally do feels strange at first.

No Leaning

When you walk up hills or stairs, the unconscious tendency is to lean forward. That is what most people do. That is slumping.

When you lean forward, your lower back changes from its powerful concave (inward) curve to a straight spine. Seen from a side view, a straight spine represents a 100 percent loss of curve. That means twice as much stress and twice the potential for lower-back and knee injuries. This posture looks puny at any age.

If you continue to lean further forward, as most people do, your low back goes past straight and bows out pathologically backward (convex). Now your stress and the potential for injury to your low back and legs jump to about 250 percent more than normal. In this posture, every step traumatizes your lower body and knees. Leaning forward going up a hill or stairs looks old and decrepit. And it helps you to get that way in a hurry.

Again, look at older people who really are old and decrepit. Do you think they just now started to have that sad posture?

Walking Down Hills

When you walk down a hill, settle your weight down into your pelvis. It feels like you are starting to sit down with each step. Meanwhile, your upper body stays erect instead of leaning forward. Do not look at your feet.

You do not want to look down at your feet all the way downhill. Instead, your peripheral vision gets to see the tips of your feet, just as they are landing. Your mind memorizes the path as you go. For most of you, memorizing the hill as you go will be a new skill.

Memorizing the last few feet of the hill as your feet come to them is a skill that becomes natural very quickly. When you must look down because of obstacles, that is all right. You just do not want to be looking down at your feet the whole way down the hill or down the stairs.

When you walk down a hill looking down at your feet, your center of gravity moves up to the top of your shoulders. You are unbalanced. Having your center of gravity up around your neck is like walking down a hill with a heavy child sitting on your shoulders.

Looking down, you are top-heavy. How could you not be? Then if one of your feet slips on loose soil or leaves, your posture is so precarious that you are sliding all over the place. You can easily fall on your buttocks. Bad form.

If you look at your feet all the way downhill, you land hard on your knees with every step, *bam, bam, bam.* That is a lot of heavy trauma and insult to your knees.

If you are negotiating stairs or hills every day, leaning forward going up and looking down at your feet going down, you may believe you have chronic knee problems. You may actually have a temporary gait problem where each day, one step at a time, you are re-aggravating your knees. You'll miss your knees when they are gone.

When people behind you are walking this way, you can hear it. You do not have to look back to know they are looking straight down at their feet the whole way. If you are walking correctly while everyone around you is slipping and sliding, you remain stable.

Walking downhill correctly removes the traumatic impact from your knees. Knee problems begin to clear up by themselves. Sometimes there are weak muscles or ligaments that need to be rubbed out and misalignments that need to be realigned.

My knees used to be badly injured. A combination of chiropractic care, doing core strengthening spinal corrective exercises, good posture, and rubbing out the origin and insertion of weak muscles and ligaments brought them back to health. I know for certain how good it feels to have my knees back in good working order.

When you keep your neck and torso erect and feel like your buttocks are sitting down with each step, you are walking down a hill correctly. Then your awareness remains centered in *hara*. You feel as stable as a mountain goat. If one of your feet slides, it barely compromises your balance. Your recovery of balance is immediate, resulting in you remaining upright. You are stable. Walking downhill in this manner settles you into a state of balance that is both comfortable and quickly feels very safe.

The joy of walking returns one simple step at a time.

Walking Downstairs
Without Looking Down

Walking down stairs without having to look at your feet is exhilarating. It is incredibly elegant. You have the power. This is the way heads of state and movie stars walk downstairs when all eyes are upon them.

The first time you try to walk downstairs without looking at your feet, you will probably feel out of control. Anything that you do not normally do will feel strange at first. Most people always look at their feet on every step.

Try standing at the top of a staircase. Let your heel kick the front of the step you are standing on. Your eyes are looking out at the horizon and your torso remains erect. Now step down to the next step without looking. Then let the heel of your next foot kick the front of the step you have moved down to, and step down. Repeat this process with the next step. Walk down a few steps without looking.

Good posture energizes "bubbling wells," which are energy centers at the balls of your feet. You quickly begin to feel where your foot is on the step. Even while wearing thick-soled shoes you can feel when your foot lands in the middle of the step. Body-centered awareness is the next level of wisdom we are awakening to at this juncture in historical time.

Walking down a flight of stairs while you are looking forward, and not having to look down when you step off of a curb, give you an amazing feeling of empowerment. Try it. Keep expanding the number of steps you can walk down without looking down. Your body will feel the thrill when you can walk down an entire flight of stairs without having to look down. It is exciting—like the pleasure you had as a child just doing simple movements. Remember?

CHAPTER 24

Lift Your Buttocks Up
When You Walk

Now we are getting to the good stuff. There is a thrill in your body when you walk and move like a superb athlete. You can move the same way, even if you are not super-conditioned.

Lift up your buttocks when you walk. Tighten up your buttocks and your thigh muscles as you walk. This makes all of your muscles and ligaments work together, lifting you up into the promise of yourself. The base of your skull is pushing ever upward. You are breathing out forcefully from *hara*. When you do this, you feel the thrill of your body, the sensuous pleasure as it is propelled through space by all of your muscles working in concert.

Imagine that your feet are pulling the ground toward you with each step. Your feet are parallel. All of your muscles and ligaments participate with each step. Lift up your buttocks as you move forward with one leg and then the other.

You can even imagine the air is more like water, and your arms are pulling you forward as if you are swimming. This gives you a catlike feeling of moving through space with your upper body.

You are "alive" to this moment. You have an intimate awareness of the space around you. Your body feels expansive. You experience the profound sensation of "knowing" the entirety of your body in the same instant. Every part of your body feels alive. There is no other moment but this moment. Your mind ceases its chatter.

You move like a tiger. This is how cats move. Your body floats through space, pushed along by a force unknown yet vaguely familiar. This is like the magic you felt as a child, exhilarated doing simple movements, feeling the thrill of an alive body. All of your muscles and ligaments propelling you along, floating in the joy of pure movement . . .

Try this experiment. First, lift up fully into your muscles. Lift your buttocks up when you walk. Move around like this for awhile. Feel yourself being propelled, floating in space. All your muscles are fully participating as you walk. You are pulling the ground toward you with each step and lifting your buttocks up. You are in the flow.

Remember how it feels to move this way.

Settling Into Your Bones: Gravity Wins

Now do the second part of this exercise. Allow yourself to settle down into your bones and walk around the room. Move the way you usually do. The usual way of walking probably has you settling down into your bones. You walk heavily down into your feet.

Can you feel the arches of your feet flatten down? Settling down into your bones, the movements are tiring and, well—pathetic. As your arches flatten it causes your great toes to slowly displace inwardly, toward your other toes. Settling down into your bones causes this foot problem.

Lifting up into your buttocks, the movements are exciting. Notice the difference in these two styles of simple movement. What a difference!

Sadly, most people settle down into their bones as they move from one place to another. No wonder most people park as close as they possibly can and begrudge the short distances they have to walk.

Take a Walk Like This

Go for a walk while lifting your buttocks the whole way. Walking like this feels so wonderful. You have got to give this a shot.

Enjoy the toned-up feeling of enlivened muscles and ligaments for the whole walk. Feel your head come up over your collarbones and settle down behind them as your forehead rocks forward. Your throat relaxes. *The back of your skull always feels like it is being pushed upward.*

Practice breathing out forcefully from your lower abdomen. You become aware of all of your ligaments and supporting fasciae fully toned up and participating. You feel like you are propelled by the purity of your design. You feel like you are floating.

It is easy to forget and go back to the way you have always moved through life. It is so, so easy to forget. *Remember how good this feels. Keep returning to this way of moving through life.*

Enjoy your body. In your whole life, your body is the finest thing you will ever own. Your body is hardwired at birth for infinitely more capabilities than you can possibly integrate, even if you go for it as intently as you can during your entire lifetime.

Your body has so much joy for you to discover. Every year you can feel more powerful, more alive than you did the year before. Every year you can be healthier, more aware of your feelings. You log more time living in the here and now. This is living at the upper limits of your life. The upper limits are where you will find all the fun and joy.

CHAPTER 25

Is Your Beltline Horizontal?

A few years ago I was watching a major golf tournament on television. All of the front-runners had great posture. I was impressed that all the golfers kept their beltlines perfectly horizontal to the ground—all but one. His belt buckle aimed at the ground a few feet in front of him.

As I was wondering how a professional golfer could be in the front running with such obviously bad posture, the commentators began discussing him. "How good it is to see him in the top running," one said. "When he's hot, he's exciting to watch." The other agreed but added, "The trouble is that he has a tendency to be inconsistent."

Mastery of golf, or any highly competitive sport for that matter, requires near-perfect posture. Talent will only take you so far. To get to the level of mastery, you must develop the fundamentals. Abdominal breathing and posture are the most basic of the absolute fundamentals of a high-quality life.

You may not aspire to be a world-class athlete, but better posture each and every year than you had the year before gives you more control and enjoyment in everything you do. All your movements become more joyous. You recapture the pure pleasure you had as a child doing something as simple as walking.

As you practice breathing out forcefully from your abdomen (breathing in is passive), your weight naturally centers above that big knob (called the "malleolus") at the side of your ankles. This posture strengthens your arches.

When you first attempt standing erect with your beltline horizontal, it feels like you will fall over backwards. That is because most people position their upper-body weight way out over their toes. That is called "sway-back." Your hips sway out over your toes, which works better for jumping or the push-off stage at the end of your stride. This posture makes all of your lower body muscles and ligaments get out of balance.

When you lean forward, the entire weight of your body compresses your toes. That flattens your arches. Your toes are not made for weight bearing. It is no wonder that so many people have flat feet.

After enough years of having your weight out over your toes, your great toes can start misaligning inward (pressing toward your other toes). That makes your feet look deformed. You can prevent this foot problem and correct it to some degree by making a habit of lifting up your buttocks when you walk.

Most people's posture, breathing, and diet get worse as they age. Then they call it old age. As you stand and move in correct posture, your arches begin to form back up toward their normal healthy state. All things improve with time. Your body is constantly changing. These habits empower and vitalize your body more each year as you age.

CHAPTER 26

The Art of Balance

Correct posture gives your balance impeccable feedback. Half of your sense balance comes from the semicircular canals of your ears. The other half comes from a vast plexus of sensory nerves that give feedback from the muscular tonus of your legs, torso, and neck. These two systems work together to give you an integrated sense of balance.

Your balance is always getting better or getting worse. No function in your body ever just "stays the same." Your balance improves as your posture improves. Incorrect posture causes your balance to deteriorate. Aging with bad posture causes the feedback of your balance system to become quite compromised.

You are held erect by the law of opposition, which is a precise system of muscles opposing each other. Bad posture gives unbalanced feedback from your ligaments and muscles. Weak muscles, muscles that underperform when you let gravity push you down, do not make enough nerve energy. That requires the opposing muscles to compensate by working harder. Overworking, they put out too much nerve energy.

Your body's innate intelligence always does the best it can. However, bad posture creates a steadily worsening feedback situation. The nerves that are forced to work too hard constantly fire off too many impulses. That really freaks out your nervous system. Your central nervous system cannot tolerate nerves constantly making that much noise. That would be like someone following you around yelling all the time.

That forces your nervous system to dampen the "hot" nerve feedback coming from your overly tight muscles to give you peace of mind. Thus, bad posture forces your central nervous system to basically dumb down. As a result, your awareness of balance deteriorates—slowly, insidiously.

Now, when you start to fall, your dampened neuromuscular feedback system fails to recognize that you are falling until you have listed too far. Then it overcompensates in its attempt to prevent you from falling. Movements become jerky and progressively unsteady. As bad posture further dampens your feedback system, you develop a (frank) loss of balance. This is not old age. This is simply bad posture.

When you get to senior citizen status (it happens faster than you think), loss of balance becomes a major issue. After years of bad posture, older people begin to fall more often.

When you get older, you do not bounce near as well as you did when you were a kid. Bones break more easily. They do not mend as quickly. Surgeries to repair broken bones on older people, and the time they are laid up, create quite an immune challenge. Many never recover. Loss of balance is a disaster. This is a predictable result of bad posture.

At any age, posture can be corrected. For those of you who are older, a number of large studies have consistently shown that "old dogs can learn new tricks." It is just as easy to learn new things when you are older as it was when you were young. Young people (of all ages) know that anything they commit to is possible.

Many "old" people have already thrown in the towel. They have a futile rationale. For them, change is not possible. It is too late. I find it interesting that healthy people look for ways to be healthier. The people who most need help are the least likely to seek it.

As soon as you start having better posture and a better gait, your neuromuscular feedback system begins to respond. Balance returns. The better your posture, the better your balance. How would you like to walk down a railroad track for long distances without falling off?

How Bad Posture Alters Your Bones

Incorrect posture progressively forces your bones out of their normal alignment. All your bones react to a law called "the piezoelectric effect," which is the physics of crystals. Your bones are made up of crystalline materials and function as crystals.

Any unequal pressure to any bone (or crystal) will cause it to develop a positive and a negative pole just like a magnet. You really do not want positive and negative polarities to build up in your bones. They create unhealthy force fields. You may have seen an illustration of a force field surrounding a magnet.

When a bone misaligns, the part of the bone that gets jammed against another polarizes into a negative force field. The negative force field immediately starts attracting calcium into all the tissues that are within its influence. Calcium has a positive electrical charge. On X-rays you can see the calcium that is attracted into the negative force field around a misaligned bone. In the early stages of a misaligned (subluxated) vertebra, the calcium buildup looks like clouds where the misalignments are. This is how arthritis occurs. Regular chiropractic care helps you to keep your spine and extremity bones in correct alignment.

Because of the piezoelectric effect, any misaligned bone immediately begins making arthritis. Good posture starts getting rid of arthritis. Spinal twists, where you put your elbows out and twist left and right fifteen times gently, work a day's worth of arthritic build-up out of your spine every time you perform them.

What medical doctors and some chiropractors call "degenerative disc disease" is simply the discs between your vertebrae becoming dehydrated. On MRIs they call dehydrated discs "desiccated discs." Desiccated means dehydrated. The spinal twists also rehydrate all of the discs between each vertebra every time you do them.

Calcium buildup in the tissues around a misaligned bone is like sand. With every movement, it irritates the muscle and nerve tissues it infiltrates. This causes inflammation and pain. If the misalignment continues because you keep doing stuff in the same old bad posture, that calcium cloud builds into arthritic spurs on the misaligned bones.

The longer you have the bad posture, the worse the spurs will get. You lose your range of motion. Old age or hard physical labor gets the blame.

There is good news.

As soon as you start having good posture and walking with a correct gait, the force fields (created by the pressure of your misalignments) fade away. When this happens, the spurs and arthritic build-up start disappearing. Every time you perform the spinal twists you work a day's worth of arthritic build-up out of your entire spine. You have to sustain your bad posture and incorrect gait if you want to keep your arthritis. Your bones are continuously changing for the better or for the worse. Time is the scorekeeper.

CHAPTER 27

How Do You Pick Things Up?

All through the 1970s and 1980s, a Russian power-lifter named Alexei Alexious dominated the Olympics. He maintained perfect posture while lifting. He successfully defended his world champion status year after year until he was thirty-five years old in a sport where you are completely over the hill by the time you are twenty-four. That would be like a fifty-year-old quarterback in the NFL. This is how he did it.

He kept his feet parallel. They were always exactly the width of his hips apart, while the rest of the power-lifters kept their feet wide apart and toed out. Most of them still do. He stuck his buttocks out backwards as far as he possibly could when he dropped down to lift.

He never lost the concave curve in his low back. His torso was erect. I watched in awe. Few people are anywhere near as flexible as this strongman who could lift up the rear end of my car.

He never varied from perfect posture. Those habits kept him injury-free and at the top of the field of Olympic power lifters while others came and went—due to injuries.

Just as the advances in automobile racing find their way into domestic automobiles within a year or two, the lessons of Olympic power lifters can help you in all the daily lifting you do.

- ○ Ninety percent of your injuries come from less than one percent of your lifting.
- ○ Ninety percent of your injuries come from picking up stuff that lies below your knees, or in the trunk of your car, or from lifting things above the level of your shoulders.

It takes only a few seconds to fetch a prop or chair and place it next to a heavy object. Then you can go down onto one knee and lift the heavy object onto the prop before picking it all of the way up. To get something out of the trunk of your car, it only takes a brief moment to slide it toward you and work it up into a position where it is easier to get hold of. Jerking something up that is too awkward to lift is the problem.

When you have to put something up high (such as in a cupboard), you can grab a chair to stand on before you lift things over your head.

Preventing 90 percent of all of your injuries generally takes less than one or two minutes out of any day. That is high-quality health insurance for cheap. And, your body stays happy.

CHAPTER 28

Goal Orientation
vs. Process Orientation

Imagine a big chore like splitting and stacking a cord of firewood or spring-cleaning your house. In goal orientation you consider the job will take X amount of time, and you begin. In the real world, though, it usually takes X amount of time plus at least 20 percent more than you anticipated. The job is a chore. It is something you "have to do" before you can get to stuff you want to do. Generally you do not joyously anticipate splitting and stacking a cord of firewood or spring-cleaning your entire house.

Now consider the same job in process orientation. You are not focused on how long it will take to get the job done. Instead you are focusing on feeling happy, having a good time, being in good posture, and moving with physical prowess. During the entire process you are lifting properly and breathing properly. *You are focusing on the process, not on the goal.*

It takes about five or ten minutes to visualize performing the whole project in a joyous and efficient manner. In the firewood example, you imagine yourself splitting the wood and then stacking it. When you see yourself moving or lifting incorrectly, you rewind the tape like a movie and run it again, lifting correctly. You rerun the scenes as many times as it takes until you do each part of the job in good posture. You are keeping your feet parallel when you are lifting, even when one foot is forward of the other; you are sticking your buttocks out and keeping your torso erect when you lift.

When you are splitting the wood, your feet are also parallel. You breathe out forcefully as the splitting maul hits the wood. The wood splits each time you swing. Ah! That is so gratifying.

Having a good time during the project is important. If you start getting uptight, you back the tape up and ask yourself, "Why am I frustrated?" When you ask the right questions, you receive revelations about your own unique process that were previously latent.

When you can see yourself doing the entire job with good posture—lifting correctly in each portion of the project, breathing out with each downward swing of the maul—and when you have imagined yourself having a good time during the entire job, you are ready to begin.

All the while you are visualizing the process, your mind efficiently organizes every aspect of the whole job. You barely take one extra step, yet you get done 20 percent ahead of your anticipated schedule.

Every part of your body, mind, and spirit gets to participate. After you are done, your body feels buffed. The whole process is joyous. The job becomes sacred, and your house reflects that sacred feeling back to you.

Do the math about the time the project takes, and also the chemistry regarding your moods. Goal-orientation tasks consistently take 20 percent longer than you anticipate. You feel abused by the job. You are not thrilled by the outcome. The job does not feel like it is going to win you any awards. You spend a lot of the time in less-than-stellar moods.

A process orientation consistently gets your projects done 20 percent sooner than you anticipate. When you compare that with taking 20 percent longer, it adds up to nearly twice as fast and a whole lot more fun. Every aspect of your body is healthier. You performed the whole project in a wonderful mood. You feel the warm glow of happiness and joy for hours afterward. You are all done, and you still have plenty of time (and energy) to stand back and admire your job. Process orientation is definitely the way to go.

Under goal orientation, the job felt like a chore you "had to do." *In process orientation the mundane becomes sacred.* You are in the moment throughout the entire project. You glimpse how "this" is the answer to all your prayers for as far back as you can fathom. You feel high for hours afterward.

Either everything you do is sacred or nothing is. There is a delightful Buddhist saying, "Before enlightenment, chop wood, carry water. After enlightenment, chop wood, carry water." When everything is done as if this moment is what your whole life was designed for, then all of life becomes joyous. Every moment is sacred. This is the life you are meant to have. You live your life in the upper limits. And your upper limits keep expanding, presenting you with greater possibilities and higher potentials. Your life fulfills its promise. You are the one you seek. You always were.

○ **Practice breathing out forcefully from your lower abdomen** as often and as much as you can until it becomes your normal habit of doing things. This keeps your back and stomach muscles balanced.

○ **Keep your feet parallel**, no matter what you are doing.

○ **Allow your torso to lengthen and broaden**.

○ **Relax your shoulders**. As your shoulders relax they become a stable yet flexible platform for your neck and head.

○ **The back of your skull is always pushing upward**. If you had a miner's lantern on your forehead, its beam would be bouncing along about 45 feet in front of you.

Your low back has two opposing rules:

❖ *Rule 1: When you stand or walk on flat ground, tuck your buttocks down. Your belt buckle aims straight toward the horizon.*

❖ *Rule 2: For everything other than standing or walking on flat ground, stick your buttocks out backward.*

These two rules keep your low back curvature in a healthy concave state under all of the different circumstances of your life.

General rules:

○ **Pick everything up as if it weighed as much as you could possibly lift.**

○ **90% of your injuries are caused by 1% of your activities and are easily prevented.**

Walking up hills:

○ **Keep your head and body erect. Stick your buttocks out.**

Walking down hills or stairs:

○ **Breathe out forcefully from your lower abdomen. Look at the horizon.** With each step your buttocks move downward as if you are starting to sit down. If you pay attention, you can feel where your feet are on the step, even with thick sole shoes.

CHAPTER 29

The Five Elements

The Physiology of the East:
A Holistic Model

When I was first introduced to the "five elements," I was moved to tears. Finally, I'd discovered a system that embraced my wholeness. It was like coming home. The five elements embrace all of our little oddities and eccentricities. I find myself so grateful for my body and for the blessing of this human experience.

The five elements is an understanding of physiology developed by the Chinese over a continuum of five thousand years. Each dynasty added its contribution as the science of acupuncture expanded to include new discoveries. Chinese physiology ties together the physical, mental, emotional, and spiritual aspects of body function in a grounded way.

Medical physiology, which developed in the West, is half of the truth about how your body works. Chinese physiology is the other half. They are like the two sides of a clamshell. When you put the two systems together, you gain a more complete and balanced perspective of physiology.

The ancient Chinese saw everything as a manifestation of the One, which they called *Tao*. The One is that which precedes being, precedes existence, contains all things and underlies all reality. All things remain connected to, and are supported by, the One. Without the unconditional love that emanates from the One, creation cannot exist.

The One manifested into what we call reality by dividing into polarities. The ancients called these polarities *yin* and *yang*. Shamans and mystics call the world of polarities (the world we can see) *Maya*, the great illusion. Quantum physicists also observe that the world we see is an illusion.

In Chinese physiology the starting point of everything is the One, not the many. We connect to the One through *qi,* the vital force that animates all life. Westerners would probably call this vital force the "holy spirit." *Qi* is in a constant state of change. Its patterns of movement create and sustain all living beings.

We can observe the patterns of *qi* operating through the five elements of wood, fire, earth, metal, and water. The five elements can be seen throughout nature and the universe. They can also be seen as the principle forces operating through your body. Within your body, each element has one or more "officials" who supervise the functioning of the life force within that particular element.

The Officials: Supervisors of Your Life Force

Your officials are much like wise governors who rule in the spirit of unconditional love, truth, and commitment. Working cooperatively, they sustain your sense of purpose, growth, and fulfillment.

An official is much more than just an organ. Each official includes the muscles that make energy for that organ and the meridians (or vessels) that connect the whole organ system together with ever-smaller, duct-like vessels—all the way down into the nucleus of every cell.[1] The energy flowing through the meridians expands until it fills all of the space within your body. The energy of the meridians continues pushing outward until it forms your auric field (also called the aura). The energy from your meridians could very well be what you consider consciousness.

---

1 The science of applied kinesiology contributed the knowledge that each organ has a specific group of muscles that makes the energy it requires.

When an official is not able to perform its duties, you experience disease, which over time can evolve into disease. Disease begins when you "get out of truth" with the simple functions of your officials. As you come back into truth, your healing manifests from within and moves outward. Time keeps score. The way of health is simple. The simplicity is the great mystery.

Disease, if you choose to focus on it, becomes progressively more complex the more you study it. Your physical body is a temporary vehicle that allows your spirit to experience a multidimensional life. This body you get to live in is a precious gift, no matter what you might think of it. From a spiritual perspective, your body is a seven-dimensional hologram. Your body is a vehicle for your consciousness.

You need to keep heart, mind, and will in balance:

○ The heart issue is to cherish others and feel your feelings.
○ The mind issue is to tell the truth, act honorably, and manage your thoughts as if everyone can hear them.
○ The issue of will is to commit to what you know when you know it. Be decisive.

Your life's work is keeping these three values in balance. They are the three-way foundation upon which you stand.[2]

When you fail to cherish people, tell the truth, or commit to what you know, the court of your officials can become a place of clashing personalities and varying temperaments. Your officials, distracted by the pain and suffering they are holding onto, may begin to act against your best interests. Things can spiral out of control when you lose your sense of purpose.

---

2 Steiner, Rudolph. *How to Know Higher Worlds.* (Steiner Books, 1994.)

Westerners typically want to stop creation so we can dissect it. We want to break things down to their smallest possible components. Once we get down to a thing's basic building blocks, we believe we can then dissect and understand it. This type of concrete, linear thinking limits our view of reality to just the physical and mental realms. There are many dimensions beyond these, which are only two pieces of the pie called reality.

The Chinese considered transformation and change (not cells and atoms) as the building blocks of life. The way something manifests (from the One or from you) is by dividing into polarities of *yin* or *yang*. The characteristics of *yin* or *yang* are female or male, cold or hot, solid or hollow, and thousands of other contrasting distinctions. Everything is divided into *yin* and *yang*. These qualities are not static, but in a constant state of change. When something has become as *yang* as it can, it begins transforming into *yin*; transformation and change are the only constants.

Transformation and change can serve you well. Every step you take toward wholeness is rewarded by a factor of ten. Improve your posture, and each year your bones remodel into cleaner, more functional shapes. Poor posture deforms your bones more each year and makes them arthritic. Breathing out from your lower abdomen empowers every part of who you are, and the empowerment increases every year. Thinking in harmony with the simple way your officials function brings your physiology into harmony. Age empowers you. Health embraces you. A powerful life welcomes you. It just keeps getting better.

CHAPTER 30

The Element of Wood

Your Splendid Plans and Dreams

The ancients likened the element of wood to a new shoot pushing up through the hard earth. Your splendid goals, dreams, hopes, plans, and ideals are in many ways like new shoots pushing up through the hard earth in the springtime. So full of promise. Such potential. So delicate. So vulnerable. Nurturing a new shoot until it can fend for itself is comparable to nurturing a new dream or goal until it becomes established.

Figuring out what you want is by far the most difficult part of manifesting your desires. Then when you have figured out what you want, you must commit to it. Commitment is like putting your car into gear. Manifesting is easy once you know and commit to what you want.

The instant you commit, anger completely transforms into one of the heartfelt emotions such as certainty in your dream, gratitude, or thankfulness. No trace of anger remains. The clearer and higher you can focus the vibration of your heartfelt emotions, the more powerfully your desires are attracted toward you.

Sometimes it is better to get forgiveness than permission. When you first start to do something, usually you do not know exactly how it will turn out. You want a life of action, not a life of holding back. Give yourself permission to make mistakes—even big ones. Doing one thing really stupidly teaches you more than you can learn doing a thousand things right. Mistakes are your true teachers. Let them guide you to your desires; you do not want to die with your songs still in you.

The driving energies of the wood element are hope, vision, future, vitality, exuberance, birth, growth, activity, and regeneration. These qualities exist outside of us and within us. As above, so below. When your wood element is healthy, you can feel the noisy exuberance of your plans and dreams wanting to bust out from within your being. You have vision. You have a bold future to manifest into being. You want to shout it out. Nothing can stop you.

The emotion associated with the element of wood is anger, although many forms of anger are not associated with this element. The anger coming from your wood element needs to burst out. It is vigorous and forceful, a feeling that wants to shout. When you block that kind of energy, you become frustrated, hostile, and resentful. However, indulging your anger by letting yourself stay mad about something is counter-productive. Staying angry harms your liver.

If you indulge your anger by staying angry, or if you suppress this vigorous energy, less honest emotions come forward, such as feeling powerless or galled. When you assume that something outside yourself is blocking your plans or dreams, the blocked energies emerge from you less honestly in the form of stubbornness, depression, or irrational behaviors. These secondary emotions are how you rationalize giving up your dreams and goals. They can appear to be part of your personality—temporarily, or for your whole life if you actually believe someone or something out there controls your destiny.

You can spend years indulging your anger or rationalizing some combination of these secondary emotions. Indulging anger in no way helps you to get what you want. Anger is your source of power, but only when you learn to direct it.

The type of anger your liver produces gets you out of your rut. It pushes you to assert the action that accomplishes your goals. When you become angry, you need to slowly look around the circle of your life, as if you are doing a slow turn until you spot what is irritating you. When you find it, that is where you need to work.

CHAPTER 31

Liver: The Architect of Your Life

Your liver official gives you a sense of purpose. It has been called the general in charge of strategic planning. You can have great levels of distress if you can see no future or no growth in your life. When you commit to a plan, your liver takes in enough energy to accomplish that plan. No plan, no energy—and no future.

What you are encountering this week, this month, is the fruit of your beliefs—what you are talking about with your friends. If you believe, or are talking about lack, your liver is drawing up plans for more lack to come into your life. As you lament the lack you feel, your heart is developing insights into how to get more lack into your life. You get as much lack as you talk about and focus your thoughts and feelings on. Is lack what you want?

Your liver listens in on all your thoughts, feelings, attitudes, and beliefs. It observes what you focus upon. Based on those observations, it draws up the plans that create the exact world you have been focusing your attention upon. Put a watcher up there in your mind. Observe what your mind is focusing on. Ask yourself dozens of times a day if what you are thinking or feeling is how you want to create your world.

Your liver and gall bladder are like blood brothers who work better together than they ever could separately. Your liver is the architect of the world on which you focus. You are a creator, with a little "c"; you create your own world. No two individuals live in the same world. One of life's great mysteries is how each person's world coincides with every other person's world. You are only responsible for the world you create—or fail to create.

Springtime is the season of wood. "It is the time of birth and regeneration," says acupuncturist and writer J. R. Worsley.[1] Professor Worsley introduced the five elements into the West. "The burst of activity surges out of the stillness of winter with no equal elsewhere in the year. The activity is noisy and exuberant. Seeds thrust their way through the earth with astonishing strength."

Activity expresses upward in a flexible and purposeful manner. There is order to it. It follows a blueprint contained within the seed. The vigorous growth force of the element of wood is an exquisite quality of life that we get to experience.

So, truth for you is the answer to the question, "Is this how I want to create my world?" If "this" is not the way, then it is not your truth. Truth is completely personal.

Your gall bladder faithfully constructs the plans your liver develops. If you are thinking about what you like and you are feeling happy about what you have, you are creating the world of your hopes and dreams. If you are focusing on what you *do not* like, that is the world your liver and gall bladder officials are manifesting. Notice what you feel when you think about your plans and dreams. Negative feelings push your dreams away; positive feelings attract your dreams to you. If you have a negative feeling about one of your plans, you need to realistically confront that feeling. If you cannot overcome that negative feeling, it will shape your destiny. Do not just leave it hanging there.

Your liver also makes the plans that all your other officials use in their functions. A healthy liver grants flexibility to your ligaments and muscles as well as to your mind, heart, and spirit. Each official's healthy functioning is interdependent upon the contribution of every other official.

1 Worsley, J. R. Classic *Five-Element Acupuncture: The Five Elements and the Officials.* (1998, Redwing Book Co.) Professor Worsley is credited with introducing the five elements into Western culture.

CHAPTER 32

Gall Bladder

Your gall bladder functions like the general contractor that constructs every one of your liver's plans. That goes for all your bodily functions as well. The architect makes the plans, but it takes the contractor to turn those plans into reality. Your gall bladder official makes all the long range and split-second decisions and judgments about your plans and dreams.

When I started my first year at Palmer Chiropractic College they loaded what semed like the six most difficult anatomy courses into the first quarter. At the end of the third week the first hour professor announced that "starting next week we will be adding a three unit terminology course—one hour prior to the start of this class." Students were still grumbling about it three weeks later.

I realized that I wanted to know the Latin suffixes, prefixes, and root words for my whole life. As soon as I committed to the additional class, my liver began uptaking enough energy to handle the additional load. No commitment, no energy. Being decisive—committing to the lessons that come at you—is one of the seven simple habits that profoundly change your life. Your gall bladder also makes good judgments about your plans' worth. It allows you to see to the heart of ideas and thoughts so you can identify the rights or wrongs that lie within. This allows you to think clearly. To the exact degree that you fail to decide about the little things in your life, or commit to what you know, your gall bladder's ability to convert your splendid dreams and plans into reality is diminished. Commit to what you know and you get what you desire. It is not that complicated.

Problems with any official occur when you have lack—or excess. You can err on the side of not showing good judgment, or on the other extreme of making everyone's decisions for them. You can fail to decide, or consider a decision infallible as if no mere human can change it. That is when compassion goes out the window.

When you are indecisive, you lose control of your world. Others wind up creating your world for you. You are no longer the lead actor in your own movie. You let others decide your purpose.

CHAPTER 33

The Element of Fire:
Learning to Cherish

Cherishing others brings you into harmony with the essence of the fire element. Life is all about choices. Moment by moment you have the power to choose. There are no victims and no injustice, but it is possible to focus on injustice, victimization, or controlling others. Everyone is exactly where he or she needs to be to learn his or her lessons. You can worry about others, and try to fix them, or any number of other dramas. Or, you can cherish others.

There are no one-way thoughts in the universe. Every thought elicits a response. Think angry thoughts at another, and that person's response back to you will tend to be either a similarly angry thought or a defensive one. Cherish them and they tend to cherish you back.

The upward, surging growth of the element of wood makes a subtle shift and slows down as we move into the cycle of summer. The element of fire directs love and warmth outward toward fruition.

Flowers and fruits blossom into a blaze of colors, fragrances, and tastes that inspire pure joy and fun within every being. As the days lengthen, the warmth of unconditional love helps everything achieve its potential.

The warmth of unconditional love makes the fluids and sap flow. It helps everything to flow on all levels, including the exchange of ideas and feelings. The fire element fills your body, mind, and spirit to overflowing with joy. The abundance of love and warmth naturally wants to go out to others. We feel our interconnectedness with others and with all of nature.

The element of fire influences everything and everyone to achieve ripeness and maturity. There is so much beauty and goodness. The fire element fills every living being with warmth and love. That love is given unstintingly. It permeates every part of your body, mind, and spirit.

However, this love is given in appropriate measure, just as the growth inspired by the element of wood stays within appropriate boundaries. If there is not enough love, nothing can push out to fruition. If there is too much or too long a season of warmth, we have drought. Plants wither. People do, too. Reservoirs dry up. If the warmth is not regulated, it can scorch and destroy life. The boundaries and limits that are created by the heart official protect and nurture us.

A bountiful harvest from the element of earth in late summer depends on the proper amount of warmth from the fire element. There is a definite plan. All the cycles of life depend on the spirits of the five elements operating in harmony. So it is within us as well. As we come into harmony with the operating rules of the five elements, life starts making sense. It keeps getting better.

Part of bringing yourself into harmony with the spirit of the fire element is to remain in the moment by bringing your attention back to what you love and your splendid plans and dreams, as if they currently existed. When you focus on those, your heart provides insights that make the world a more loving place. Cherishing others is more healing to the world than spending your energies protesting what is bad. Consistently choosing to love is the real revolution.

Sixty percent of what a woman focuses on tends to be "the relationship." Sixty percent of what a man focuses on tends to be his plans and dreams. Each one needs to lovingly keep their focus on their values instead of dissipating their precious attention on worries, problems, or fretting about what someone else says or does.

When you focus on cherishing others, it keeps you in harmony with the element of fire within yourself. Your face and eyes brighten. Your mind lights up. You are filled with enthusiasm. You have the capacity to laugh. Others can hear it in the tone of your voice.

Choosing to love is one of the seven habits that change your life. Cherish yourself. Cherish others—including the jerks—and cherish your splendid plans and dreams. Everything else is a distraction.

The Dalai Lama, who is one of the brightest spiritual lights on the planet at this time, believes "the purpose of life is to cherish others."[1] He also said, "When I cherish others, they tend to cherish me back. When they cherish me back, it makes me feel so good inside that I cherish others for purely selfish reasons." If your heart could speak, this is surely what it would say. The Dalai Lama provides us with the most perfect example of how an emperor can be. He even loves those Chinese leaders who directed their subordinates to kill or torture millions of his people.

---

1 *The Dalai Lama Speaks Out on Religion*, a booklet published by Snow Lion Publications about ten years ago.

CHAPTER 34

Your Heart is the Emperor
of Your World

You manifest your own world into being by what you focus on, and your heart functions as the emperor in that world. All your other organs are considered governors. Your heart rules the governors and all of your individual cells by loving them completely and unconditionally.

Every cell and organ is completely dependent on the warmth of love that comes from your heart. Without that love they cannot grow or mature to their potential. Without your heart focusing its love upon them, neither your cells nor your splendid plans and dreams can come to fruition.

The ancient Chinese called the heart official the "supreme controller." They did not use words like "supreme" or "great" lightly. Your heart is the closest thing to God you will find in your body. The qualities we attribute to God are the qualities your heart represents. It can be thought of as the root of life itself, the residence of spirit.

When the love of your heart focuses on distractions, your cells and organs and your plans and dreams suffer. They are like apple trees that should be producing hundreds of juicy red apples, but instead can only produce fifteen or twenty paltry apples in a season. The unconditional love that your heart grants to its subjects personifies the finest qualities of your spirit.

As your heart loves every cell and organ, it develops insights. Based on the insights that come from unconditional love, your heart issues the operating rules your cells and organ officials need so they can bring their particular issues to fruition. As a human, of course, you are not rooted to the ground like a tree. You can find yourself in different environments from one day to the next. In the ever-changing environments, all of your cells and organs depend on your heart for its insights that give them healthy limits and boundaries. The very life of each official and cell depends on the insights, limits, and boundaries the heart official continually establishes.

All of your cells and your organs take whatever you are thinking or feeling personally. They believe that whatever thoughts or feelings you are projecting outward are actually aimed inwardly at them. Muscle testing absolutely confirms this. Anger or fear projected outward rebounds inward with terrible consequences. Your body suffers immensely from any negativity you project outward. Cherishing yourself, your plans and dreams, and others is the preferred background for every thought or action.

Your entire body's health depends on you cherishing others. Forgive. Accept what is. Spend more time forgetting the unpleasant things of the past or fears of the future. The past and future have no form or substance other than what you give them. There is only now. Letting your awareness believe that the past or future has any power over you is the principle cause of pain and suffering in your life.

When you think about a future event or possibility, what you feel and believe is the part that is real. The same goes for the past. The more you love, the greater your attraction is to the things you want. The more concern you feel, the more you push your splendid plans and dreams away.

Each person creates his or her own unique world, for which your heart reigns as emperor or empress. Since you are creating your own world, why not imagine a world where each day more people learn to cherish each other? Imagine a world where each day, more people wake to put their piece into the great puzzle of life.

Everyone stands on a different rung of Jacob's ladder. They are all doing the best they can. What they reflect upon and believe is what each one of them creates. The world each person sees is a direct reflection of what he or she believes. You are only responsible for what you personally create. Create the love you want by loving what you have. Then your heart develops insights to have more of that.

When your heart is healthy, your eyes are bright, and you are filled with enthusiasm and joy. You have clear boundaries. Work is a source of pleasure. Goals and tasks are a source of fun, no matter how difficult or tedious they may be. Actually, we crave challenges. You may choose to have your difficulties be the intricacies of your splendid goals and dreams. That is a lot better than projecting that something or someone out there is blocking you.

Your heart cannot unconditionally love its subjects and provide insights that lead to rules while simultaneously defending itself. Those are mutually exclusive directions. Because of this, your heart has three imperial bodyguards whose primary duty is to keep your heart focused on what you love and the world you want to manifest. That way your heart is providing the unconditional love and insights that all its subjects, and all of its splendid plans and dreams depend upon.

The three officials covered in the following section also serve as ambassadors, providing they never forget their primary function. Their primary function as imperial bodyguards is to prevent distractions that take your heart away from providing its love and attention to its primary duties. Consciousness concerns 99.99 percent of all health issues—and diseases. Understanding the simple operating rules of each imperial bodyguard safeguards your ruler so he or she can create your kingdom and keep it safe.

CHAPTER 35

Small Intestine

Imperial Bodyguard to the Heart

Your small intestine's primary function is to protect your heart. It is one of the three imperial bodyguards whose primary function is to prevent distractions from getting to your heart. You really hamper your well-being when you continually focus your awareness on the things you do not like, things you really need to let pass on by. Every time your heart has to sort out—again—a bad thing that happened, it is distracted by the nonproductive issue you brought it. During that time your heart is unable to give everyone the love and insights they need. Days can slip by while your heart (the emperor) is too distracted to provide the love and insights its subjects thrive upon.

Your heart needs the freedom to focus on what you love and your plans. That way it can provide the insights that will direct your other organ officials to manifest more of what you love, and accomplish your magnificent goals and dreams. Your heart must be protected from dwelling on foolish things.

Your small intestine official must never forget that it primarily functions as an imperial bodyguard. Its first duty is making sure that only relevant or vital (nutritional) matters are passed on to the heart. As the emperor, your heart creates the world of your desires. To do that, its imperial bodyguards must keep trivial or disrupting matters out.

Your small intestine's ability to sort things out helps you make sense of everything in your environment. This is where your natural sense of justice forms. As you might imagine, this function depends on the interconnectedness of your gall bladder making good decisions and sound judgments, and it depends upon the warmth of love and insight from your heart. It is important to focus upon what you love instead of dissipating your life force by focusing upon what you do not like. In this way your small intestine separates the pure from the impure.

What you dwell on throughout the day is what your small intestine sends to your heart. Put a watcher up there. Become aware of what you are focusing on during the day. If you are not disciplining your mind to keep coming back to what you love and your goals, what you are most likely focusing on is a distraction. Problems are what you see when your heart is distracted from providing insights regarding your goals.

Your heart must ponder anything its three ambassadors bring it. *Because of that, each of the heart's three ambassadors—heart protector, three heater, and small intestine—must first and foremost consider themselves imperial bodyguards.*

Your small intestine's job is to let impure food (including non-nutritive thoughts, feelings, attitudes, and beliefs) pass on by. When your mind brings up an unpleasant memory you can say, "Not now." After awhile it quits bringing those memories up. That way your heart is left free to provide insights into what is pure (i.e., good about your life). As your heart ponders what is good, it provides insights into how to get more goodness.

When you eat your food in a peaceful, contemplative state, your stomach ripens the food in much the same manner as a sun-ripened tomato or peach. After your stomach has ripened the food, it passes down to the small intestine. Your small intestine takes into your bloodstream the pure aspects of the food you have eaten to nourish your body, mind, and spirit. It allows impure foods—and these include non-nurturing thoughts, feelings, attitudes, and beliefs—to simply pass on by.

The small intestine does not fight or resist non-nurturing thoughts, feelings, or attitudes any more than it resists non-nutritive foods. It simply lets them pass on by.

When you dwell upon the unpleasant parts of your life, when you keep dredging them up and reflecting on how much you do not like them, you do tremendous trauma and insult to your small intestine. Your digestion suffers, but more important, your heart is distracted. It is forced to deal with what you do not like instead of creating what you do want.

Your small intestine's job is to focus on what it cherishes and on the nourishing parts of your life. That is what you are sending to your heart. Then your heart can provide insights into manifesting more of what you cherish. Train yourself to focus upon what you love. Then your heart develops insights into how to get more of that into your life. Reflect on the good parts often, and let the non-nutritive parts of life pass on by.

Focusing on your plans and what you cherish is very healing to your small intestine. When you have forgotten the good things that happened three days ago, and instead remember all the slights that happened to you during the last six months, your small intestine suffers. Your digestion suffers. Worse, it makes your heart focus its awareness on (and use its insights to create more of) the slights that have happened to you, when it should be focusing on your plans and what you love. Put a watcher in your mind and notice what you are focusing your awareness on.

There is also a connection between your small intestine and the faculty of hearing. A healthy small intestine official grants you the power to concentrate, even when there are distractions. You distress your small intestine official by continually going back over the bad things that have happened to you. When your small intestine gets distressed, it has difficulty sorting conversations. Under distress it may not be able to sort the conversation you are trying to hear from all the background conversations or noises. This is a sorting problem, and the confusion affects your hearing.

CHAPTER 36

Circulation Sex

The Second Bodyguard in Charge of Protecting Your Heart

Circulation sex is also known as the heart protector. It does just that. It takes all the physical blows, as well as the mental and emotional traumas and shocks that would otherwise traumatize your heart. The last thing you want is for your heart to get a cramp.

There is no corollary in Western medical physiology for this system or the three-heater system. Understanding these two systems fills in an immense gap in medical physiology and contributes to a greater understanding of how your body operates.

The ingenious way this system protects your heart is by distributing the warmth of your heart's love to all of your cells and to everyone you think about. The circulation sex official (not the heart) is responsible for sending your heart's warmth and love out through the arteries to every cell in your body and bringing it back via the veins hundreds of times each day. In the higher dimensions of your consciousness, the heart protector makes possible the love between people. Unconditional love is the ultimate revolution.

Cherishing others is the primary function of your heart protector. When you cherish others, every cell in your body feels cherished. Every part of your body feels your heart's warmth and love, and is better able to rise to its duties.

Your heart protector is the ambassador to and from all of your relationships. Think about what a huge responsibility that is. Gay and Katie Hendricks are my teachers about relationship issues. In their workshops and books they define "relationship" very simply:

❍ It is where two whole people come together to share their essence.

❍ It allows the entire gamut between intimacy and aloneness.

Those two definitions are deceptively simple. They take years to master. I have logged hundreds of hours reflecting on how those two definitions have played out in personal encounters. The fruit of this effort has been incredible.

In a relationship both parties walk away with more energy than they had when they met.

When you consider people to be "whole," you are assuming that they have every skill they will ever need to handle every problem they will encounter. Assume everyone hears your thoughts. When you worry about people, what you are actually doing is diminishing them. With such logic, those people are no longer whole. Worry assumes that they are less than their problems. They become second-class citizens.

At any moment we have millions of assets. On our worst day we may have a dozen or more problems. Sometimes people get this ratio switched in their minds.

When a person wants aloneness and you completely withdraw your attention from her, a sense of peace fills the area. You have given her what she wanted. When a person needs space and you give it, magic happens. Give people the needed space and they can more quickly resolve whatever problem has arisen. You allowed them to feel safe.

You can see this with shy children or pets. When they react with shyness, and you completely withdraw all of your attention from them, invariably they become more interested in you. Who is this person that is ignoring me? Within minutes the shy child is bringing a book for you to read to them while the parent looks on incredulously.

When a person wants intimacy with you, it does not require much of it to balance the scales. But when a person wants intimacy and you push him away, you create a dysfunction that invariably takes much more energy to handle. You have created an entanglement. This may end up taking a thousand times more energy than what the person needed from you in the first place. And, unlike relationships, entanglements are never fun.

If you wonder how much intimacy or aloneness a person wants, you usually know the answer innately. A person may want 10 percent intimacy and 90 percent aloneness. Give it to her. A short time later the person may want a completely different percentage. You can feel it if you ask yourself the right question. Better questions allow the wisdom from your spirit to come to the surface of your consciousness.

Most people's encounters with others are not relationships. They are entanglements. Any encounter that does not fulfill the two definitions of a relationship is an entanglement. Entanglements suck the life out of the encounter. The undercurrents cause both parties to go away with less energy than they had.

If you observe the two simple rules of relationships, most of your encounters return more energy than you expended. Relationships bring health to your heart protector. They allow your heart protector to provide increasingly more protection to your heart. Your heart, as emperor, is in turn able to keep your kingdom safe, peaceful, and healthy. Cherishing others is the greatest protection you can give your heart.

This official, and the three heater system described below, are in a real sense pure functionaries. They represent no physical organs. The pericardium, the sack around the heart, is not really an organ. Its job is to protect the heart.

In ancient texts this system was called "circulation sex." It includes the buttocks muscles, the piriformis, and the big adductor muscles that draw your legs together. These muscles are essential for making love. All of these powerful muscles make energy for the pericardium. This should give you an idea how important the pericardium is.

CHAPTER 37

Your Body's Heating Engineer

Three Heater

Your three heater official, sometimes called the "triple warmer," is the last of the imperial bodyguards whose primary function is to keep distracting issues from taking your heart off line. Remember, one of the seven habits that change your life is to keep your focus on cherishing yourself, cherishing others, and cherishing your splendid plans and dreams.

Imagine you have doors and gates that open and close to control your warmth. When one of the gates gets jammed open or closed, your fire system can get out of balance. One of the ways you begin stabilizing this system is to not let yourself get so overly excited about an upcoming event that your doors get stuck open. You also do not want to let yourself get so depressed when things go bad that your doors get stuck closed.

When you worry, your heart has to run worst-case scenarios until it gets insights about your worries. Naturally your heart develops insights into how to create more for you to worry about. During the hours it takes your heart to sort out those problems, it's diverted from giving warmth and love to your body. All your organs that feel unloved begin to act up. During the whole time you are worrying, you often feel your "usual" symptoms acting up, due to the parts of your body that feel unloved.

Any time you wonder why a person does something that is dysfunctional, your heart must provide its insight into the logic of why that person felt justified to perform that dysfunctional act. Sometimes your heart has to work for hours just to sort out the dysfunctional thoughts and beliefs you dumped on it with a single curious question. Being curious about why anyone does anything dysfunctional is the curiosity that killed the cat. It throws your three warming spaces out of balance.

You maintain balance of your three warming spaces by a function that is like opening or closing gates. If you want to be curious about something (opening your gates), be curious about why someone you admire does what he or she does. To keep your three heater healthy, open its gates to your goals, to people and things you love, and people you admire.

Healthy regulation of the warmth of love to your body, mind, and spirit creates harmony between all your organs. It also provides love and harmony with others. Imagine a house where the temperature in all the rooms is regulated just the way you like it. There you can achieve your maximum creativity. For this reason the three heater official has been called the "heating engineer."

Your three heater official is responsible for maintaining an even balance between the three warming spaces into which your trunk is divided. The upper warming space contains the heart, heart protector, and the lungs. The middle warming space includes the liver, gall bladder, pancreas, stomach, and spleen. The lower warming space, below the naval, includes the small and large intestines, kidneys, bladder, and sexual system. The three heater maintains a comfortable balance of heat and cooling within your body relative to the varying temperatures that are occurring outside of the body.

When there is too much heat in one or more of your three warming spaces, your skin can be too hot. You can have rashes and eruptions. You feel irritated, upset, or angry. You can be pretty intense mentally and emotionally. If your energy is not focused on your plans, you can use up the people around you with your intensity. After awhile you can burn out.

When there is not enough warmth of love, you can have cold hands and feet. You can feel depressed. A weak fire element can leave one or more of your warming spaces with insufficient heat to nurture any of your plans or dreams to fruition. Your mind can feel lackluster and weary. You do not have enough energy to get excited about life or your loved ones. When your fire element lacks warmth and joy, it feels like your spirit cannot match the level of the other revelers.

When your three heater official gets out of balance, you lose the ability to keep your emotional and social thermostat in balance. You tend to blow hot and cold. These kinds of mood swings and difficulties drive friends and loved ones to desperation. When you oscillate between over-enthusiasm and indifference, it is difficult for others to maintain anything like an appropriate balance with you. This particular imbalance has sent a lot of people to counseling.

You really do not want to open the gates to why someone does something dysfunctional. A good habit is to define those kind of acts by saying, "That was inconsiderate," or whatever it was. You might add, "I do not like that." Defining it or judging it for what it is often makes you laugh because you dodged the bullet. Inwardly, you know that you did not force your heart to decipher the motives of a dysfunctional person. Wondering why anyone does anything in a dysfunctional manner puts all kinds of knots in your rope.

When your mind focuses on something you do not like, the gates naturally want to close. That is your cue to quit gawking and move along. When you persist in opening your awareness to why all the terrible things in the world are happening, you overwhelm your heart official. Your body reacts by going into an adrenal response pattern, which is called the "fright, fight, or flight response."

The news media's emphasis on sensationalism is actually quite harmful to your health. Because your body's innate intelligence takes everything personally, the sensationalism throws your body into sympathetic dominance. This is not a good thing for you. Watching the network news is hazardous to your health. Here is how. Sensing danger, your sympathetic nervous system shuts your digestive system down. It also shuts down your immune and sexual systems, all of which are superfluous when your body senses danger. The energy that otherwise would have gone to those systems is diverted to your muscles and your sense organs so you can survive the supposed threat.

When a large portion of your thoughts, feelings, and beliefs are focused on the dangers out there (which all news organizations seem to delight in serving up), or on victims or injustice, your body's response is to think that it is under attack. Remember, your body's innate intelligence takes everything personally.

When your imperial bodyguards do their jobs, you feel loved and safe. Your parasympathetic system turns your digestive system, immune system, and sexual systems back on. They get all the energy they need. You sleep well. Your body is nourished. You feel good, and you look good. When you really think about it, not feeling loved and not feeling safe are the two greatest sins of us two-leggeds.

You really want to train your mind to close the doors to what you do not like. You don't want to dwell on that kind of stuff. When you do, it diverts your heart from providing insight and effective rule over the world you want to create. Instead, your heart is kept busy trying to make sense out of the dysfunctional stuff you are focusing on.

Train your mind to keep returning its focus to everything you love. Keep redirecting your focus back to your magnificent plans and dreams. Focus on ideals that you admire. That is what you want to open the gates of your three heater to. Health, happiness, and abundance are so simple when you learn how your body operates.

CHAPTER 38

The Element of Earth

The Season of Indian Summer

The earth on which you live and the element of earth within your body provide the kind of love a mother gives her child. That love provides the foundation for feeling secure—for feeling safe and loved. A healthy element of earth ensures an abundant harvest on every level of your life, and good distribution to every part of your body, mind, and spirit.

Imagine a mother teaching her child his or her first words, being there to feed, love, offer support, and provide security and nurturing for the child so he or she grows up to be secure and well adjusted. Home and hearth are the basis of security. Every dysfunctional thing a person does is generally the result of not feeling safe and loved.

If children do not get the support or attention they need growing up, they can become desperate. Then even as adults, these people will still be crying out for sympathy, and acting out in an attempt to get the attention they are missing. Lack of nurturing can manifest outward in a number of ways in adults.

Inadequately nurtured children may grow into adults incapable of nurturing others. All of their attention is focused on getting their own needs met. This problem can begin in early childhood, but it may also be a problem you incarnated with, something you chose to deal with in this lifetime. It is time to take responsibility for the world each of us creates.

The element of earth grants the power of sympathy. As we discussed earlier, imbalances among the elements show up as behavioral extremes. Needy people who crave the missing harvest may develop eating disorders or other attention-seeking behaviors to unconsciously try to fulfill their cravings for sympathy. These people may excessively fish for sympathy but never seem to get enough. On the opposite extreme, they might consistently give away their harvests (even though they really need it) until they fade away into martyrdom.

Or a person can become someone who wants nothing to do with sympathy—of any kind. He or she will not ask for help, and it will be rejected if it is offered. In turn, this person might not have much sympathy for others.

CHAPTER 39

Stomach

The Official in Charge of Ripening Food and Drink

Your stomach does not only consume food. It also takes in all your thoughts, feelings, attitudes, and beliefs. Your stomach official ripens these until they can nourish and provide a healthy satisfaction for your body, mind, and spirit.

You have probably tasted the difference between vine-ripened tomatoes and supermarket tomatoes, which were picked green and refrigerated until they were placed on the shelves for purchase. Tree-ripened fruit is so much tastier and nutritious than the typically green-picked fruit of the supermarket. Similarly, your stomach ripens your food before sending it to your small intestine.

You can make it difficult for your stomach official to adequately ripen what you take in when the quality of the food—or your thoughts and feelings—is poor. When you do not chew your food well or think your thoughts through, the mix is all but impossible to ripen. When negativity about a plan goes unchallenged, it can sour the food. When you process a steady diet of worst-case scenarios, you send the other officials such poor nourishment that they may reject it.

On one level, your stomach is like an internal cement mixer. As such, the finished product is a whole lot better if you put in the right mix. Seventy percent of the mix should be vegetables and fruit, the more organic the better. With very minor exceptions, fruit and vegetables are alkaline and everything else is acidic.

When your diet is mainly alkaline, your energy remains rock-solid from one meal to the next. When your diet does not include enough vegetables and fruit, you suffer midmorning and mid-afternoon energy sags.

If you consider the food you eat as fuel, you need approximately ten percent grains, ten percent proteins, and ten percent of the good fats per day. At least one-third of your fats should be omega-3 fats, which come from fish, avocadoes, walnuts, almonds, and supplemental fish, flax, borage, or evening of primrose oils. Extra virgin olive oil has the perfect ratio of one-third omega-3 fats. Your stomach takes in the mix, ripening it until the finished product can provide all the other officials with nourishment. Your bodymind also reacts to thoughts, feelings, attitudes and beliefs as if they were food. At least seventy percent of them need to originate from your heart creating a world where you are unconditionally loved and where you are safe to be who you are now—not later when you get your life together.

A small percentage of fearful thoughts, feelings, attitudes, and beliefs is healthy. My fear that this material would be too heady for people to digest influenced my need to edit and rewrite each chapter at least thirty-six times. Without a healthy level of fear this material would have come out looking like my college notes.

As you recall, your body takes everything you think and feel personally, as if these thoughts and feelings are aimed directly at your cells and officials. Dining is a sensuous experience. It sets the tone for the next four- or five-hour period when the food combined with the air you breathe is fueling your plans and desires. Focus on what you love while you eat. That way, your stomach can ripen the food before sending it down to the small intestine.

Dining is a good time for reflection and peaceful contemplation. This is a good time to be thankful for all of the goodness in your life.

Focusing on all that is undesirable while you eat causes all kinds of digestive problems. No one is immune. Naturally, sensitive people can suffer these problems sooner and more profoundly.

When your stomach does not send ripened food down, the other officials might feel like children who are not getting the love and security they need from their mother. They can feel abandoned. Remember, your stomach is part of the earth element. Earth is the archetype of mother. All of the other elements exist within the earth element.

When your stomach official is out of balance, you can suffer tremendous apprehension, depression, anxiety, or worry. The sense of apprehension can make you feel like a young child in a marketplace who has become separated from his or her mother. This sense of separation from the element of earth can make you feel so confused you do not know what is happening.

When your stomach does not ripen your food, you have difficulty getting nourishment from it. As a result, your mind tends to go blank when you are given detailed information. You may only be able to take in information when it is fed to you in small bites. Get too much information, and you cannot handle it. You may have no memory of being told something, even if you heard it a few minutes ago.

Without proper nutrition, especially for the mind and spirit, there is no connection with the earth, and no feeling of love or sympathy from the mother. You can go off on mental and spiritual trips that are unbalanced and up in the air in an attempt to reconnect with the earth.

You are a spiritual being, having a human experience. As such you are unconditionally loved and completely safe. Knowing that you are loved and safe helps you get your feet back on the ground.

When you do not feel your connection with the earth you can crave sweets and sympathy. You can be jerked around by all the feelings children have when they are hungry, tired, and lonely. The sympathy, nourishment, and sweetness that are normally offered by the mother must be developed by your stomach official. Without those qualities, you can feel so distrustful and hurt that you reject the ones you love.

The action of your stomach is sympathy. Pay attention to what you are sympathizing with. It is important to sympathize with ideas and ideals that you admire. Sympathizing with (i.e., pitying) the problems or dilemmas of others is like eating those problems or dilemmas.

There are a lot of sin-eaters out there. *You can love a person until your heart feels like it will break, but you should not feel sorry for anyone—ever.* Everyone is exactly where he or she needs to be to learn the lessons they committed to learn in this lifetime. What is happening to them is the curriculum they set up for their soul's evolution. Cherish the person or persons. Help them where you can, but do not be a sin-eater.

Disgust is a feeling that lets you know that "this" is not something you want to sympathize with. It can be a particular food. It can be something on TV, or it may be people dumping their problems on you. A lot of people think it is all right to dump their problems on others. When you keep taking them in, you are the one who ends up feeling bad. You are the sin-eater. The dumper, naturally, feels better.

To be conscious is to feel all of your feelings. The negative emotion your stomach employs to protect you is disgust. When something is disgusting to you, and you allow yourself to feel that, you also allow yourself to awaken spiritually. Then, as an aware being, you can wisely decide what you want to do. The moment you fail to feel a feeling that comes up—that moment is when you go unconscious.

If you have long-term digestive issues, then most likely you have, for a long time, stuffed emotions into your stomach that you deemed too difficult to feel. Your stomach can be so full of unresolved feelings that during stressful times, or exciting times, these feelings overwhelm you. For years, perhaps from your early childhood, you may have stuffed away unresolved depression, sadness, anger, fear, anxiety, frustration, and a host of other feelings. These unresolved feelings in your stomach cause myriad symptoms, including feelings of:

❍ Not enough time
❍ Too much to do for too little appreciation
❍ Dizziness and nausea from thinking you have too much to do
❍ Wanting to withdraw from life
❍ Long-term depression
❍ Recurring bouts of anxiety

If you have experienced a lot of anxiety or depression in your past, and you were not able to acknowledge those feelings, they may be there in your stomach. Many times a day your own stuffed feelings become activated when you encounter similar feelings in others around you.

Brush by a depressing situation, and you trigger your own library of depression. The unresolved feelings you have stuffed in your stomach can be activated by ordinary situations so often each day that it may seem like you always feel that way.

When you experience a strong feeling and you give it a story like, "I can't handle this," the feeling takes control of you. You intellectualize the feeling. Thinking a feeling is not the same as feeling the feeling. Intellectualizing, or thinking the feeling stuffs it down into your bodymind, where it continues to build up in intensity. The buildup of unfelt feelings causes, by far, most of your pain. You develop a "pain body" of built up emotional pressure.

When you experience a strong emotion and simply feel it without giving it a story, the feeling completely dissipates. Then, the next time you have that feeling, it tends to have less intensity. Feeling your feelings is the only strategy that works. Trying not to feel any feeling gives that feeling ultimate power over you. You are safe to feel these emotions because as you feel them, without giving them a story, you are releasing them.

When you give an emotion a story such as, "I am so depressed because of (some situation or person's actions)," or, "I cannot handle another anxiety attack like this," *you give that emotion control over you.* Every time you give a feeling a story, you become the victim to that particular feeling. But when you simply feel the feeling, your body releases it permanently. You have the control. The feeling no longer has any power over you.

The truth is that any feeling, whether positive or negative, that you do not feel builds up within you and causes dis-ease. As you might imagine, dis-ease over time leads to disease.

CHAPTER 40

Spleen

The Official in Charge
of Transportation and Distribution

Your spleen official can be likened to the head of a trucking company that transports and distributes the food, energy, and every other commodity that the entire population of your bodymind needs. The spleen runs trucks and delivery vehicles twenty-four hours a day, seven days a week to service every residence (cell) with everything it needs—without fail. Let us just say that our leaders are still light years from figuring out how to get good distribution to all of their citizens.

We individual citizens are still sending bad thoughts to each other. On a subconscious level, everyone is aware, to some degree, of how others feel toward him or her. Any thought you think toward another person causes him or her to have a reciprocal thought in response. So, in the unconscious state, most people walk around projecting anger and other negative feelings toward people around them. Projecting negative feelings outward shuts us off from the love that nurtures us. That causes people to be defensive and societies to be divisive.

When a critical mass of ten percent of the population awakens to the realization that, moment by moment, choosing to cherish others and consciously participating in the effort of making the world a better place will make each individual happy, then all forms of distribution will improve significantly. When you distill society down to basic desires, everyone wants the same thing. We all want to be happy, to see our children succeed, to feel fulfilled, and to have the opportunity to pursue our desires.

According to ancient texts, the spleen official also grants the five tastes, which are salty, sweet, sour, bitter, and pungent. When the spleen is healthy, you can enjoy all of the tastes nature provides. The spleen official also provides your personal tastes in clothes and the like, and your tastes regarding movies or books.

When your food has been harvested and has ripened in the stomach, it must be transported to all parts of your body soon, or else it will rot beyond healthy levels. If your stomach has not ripened the food fully, the different parts of your body will, to some degree, reject the immature food energy. As a result, you will feel hungry for something more, even after you took in enough nutrition to be satiated.

The spleen official includes both the spleen and pancreas organs and, very importantly, the meridians that run up either side of your body. It is in charge of transporting and distributing food, oxygen, blood, urine, lymph, feces, and all other substances that move throughout your body.

When any one of us stands in one spot and slowly looks around the circle of his or her life, there are millions of things to be thankful for—especially in the West. On the worst day there are rarely more than a dozen things to be resentful of. We somehow get this ratio turned around in our rational minds.

If you dislike the distribution of your life, if you feel like you do not have time to do what you want, or that you are languishing in a dead-end situation, your spleen official takes it all personally. It feels as if it has failed you.

It is not difficult to imagine your health problems if this official becomes weak and can only transport some of the commodities to some of the population. When the spleen official is weak, you cannot get enough supplies transported into your muscles. Then you cannot get all the waste products carried away quickly enough. Movement, and the motivation toward movement, becomes difficult.

When transportation to and from your nervous system is inadequate, especially to extremities such as your brain, your mental stamina and agility are diminished. It is hard to concentrate and think things through. You can feel stuck.

Your spleen official can become so immobilized from weakness that you become entrenched in your ways. It is hard to overcome the inertia and follow through with your goals. You can become the epitome of laziness, or a person who sits in a chair solving everyone else's problems, spinning thought after thought while achieving nothing for yourself. Each of us experiences each of these problems at one time or another. The trick is to not get stuck in any of these negative conditions.

Because everyone creates his or her own world, all the consequences in your life are the direct result of how you think about your world, your feelings and attitudes, and the choices you make. There are only choices and consequences, and together they create the circle of life.

How is distribution in your life? Are you making the world a better place? Do you commit to working as efficiently and productively as you can? If not, why not? Do you make time and opportunity to really play? Do you set aside enough time for contemplation? Do you have an artistic outlet? Do you sleep well? The biggest question is: Do you feel that the quality of your life has enough movement and provides fulfillment? How you answer those questions says a lot about your spleen official's health and perhaps the help you need to give it.

Taking a walk every day helps everyone. The older you get, the more you have to schedule and plan movement in your life. Join a health club. When you were a child, you naturally had lots of activity in your life. Lack of movement was never an issue. As you get older, it takes planning and commitment to get enough movement into your life. You have to make it a priority.

If you do not set aside the time for movement and action, all the essential qualities of your life suffer. Your transport and distribution systems begin to clog up. Old age usually takes the rap, but that is just ignorance.

Create your world the way you want it. Focus your awareness on making time for what you feel is important. No excuses.

CHAPTER 41

The Element of Metal

The Season of Fall

After the cycles of growth, maturity, and harvest, the cycle of life goes into decline and fall. Leaves fall to the ground and die. The air becomes heavy with mist and rain. Decaying leaves provide essential nutrients and metals for vigorous growth the following spring. Death or dying is of no use if the essential nutrients do not return to the soil.

There is usually a tinge of melancholy in the fall. Summer is over. Winter is coming. This is a time for healthy contemplation. What did you take action on this spring? Did it come to fruition? How successful was your harvest? What seeds do you want to set aside (winter) for planting next spring?

It is normal to grieve when someone or something is lost from you. Your large intestine official grants you the power of grief. But if you cannot move beyond grief, any loss hits you like a punch in the gut. Instead of living life head-on, you spend your time focusing on your rear-view mirror, thinking "if only," indulging in regrets, and wishing things were like they used to be. If you cannot let go of the past, you have no room for inspiration. You have no space to create a future, nor can you contemplate one.

This time of contemplation is important. It gives the emperor or empress—your heart—time to sit down with all his or her officials: the wood officials (liver and gall bladder), which work as architect and contractor, respectively; the earth officials (stomach, pancreas, and spleen), which oversee nourishment, harvest, and distribution; the water officials (kidneys and bladder), which give you clarity and the power to endure; and the metal officials (lungs and large intestine), which get you the life force you need to live courageously and keep everything pure by eliminating the dregs.

In a healthy, functional state, your metal officials, which connect you to your spiritual roots, are aware that this moment is the answer to all your prayers. *To the ancients, earth represents the archetype of mother, while metal represents the archetype of father.* A balanced man or woman has a healthy balance of earth and metal in their inner nature.

The finer, nurturing qualities of the earth element represent the qualities of mother—everything round, soft, nurturing, and unconditionally loving. The finer qualities of metal represent the qualities of father—everything vertical, authoritative, unbending, trusting, and wise. Your inner qualities are intimately connected with the qualities you observe in nature. Mother and father are the two biggest archetypes. If your metal element is healthy, you will have a healthy relationship with the qualities discussed in the following paragraphs.

Metal is your divine spark, the molten inner core whose pure and refined essences are so apparent in the qualities of your body, mind, and spirit. When your metal official is strong and healthy, your spirit displays the qualities embodied in the noble ideas of the father.

The father is the archetype of someone who develops the qualities of trust, wisdom, and respect. This is the type of person whose advice we will gladly follow. A person with healthy qualities of the metal element will manifest respect for others and his or her own self. Respect is an important quality of father in all cultures.

As you foster the innermost qualities of metal within yourself, you foster them in others. These qualities become part of the good judgments you weave into the tapestry of your plans. You become the best you can be.

Many of the human values linked to metal parallel those we put on precious metals and gemstones. Throughout history we have given medals for bravery as tokens of our respect. We have given precious metals and stones as evidence of our love and respect. In the healthy state, you value your self like you value an exquisite diamond and precious metals.

The element of metal is about the rhythm of taking in and letting go. Your lungs are mainly about inspiration, taking in oxygen, but also about expelling carbon dioxide.

Your lung official is responsible for taking in new things—physical, mental, and spiritual inspiration. The lungs receive energy from the heavens in the form of air, which gives all the other officials the immediate energy they need to courageously live the life you dream of—and to which you commit. Breath energy also mixes with food energy to ripen it.

Your large intestine accepts what is left over after the small intestine effectively extracts 95 percent of your nutrition. The large intestine extracts the last five percent of the minerals, absorbs enough water to firm up the stool, and then gets rid of the garbage. You must let go so there is room to take in.

If your metal official is weak, you can feel cut off from the qualities of father, cut off from the divine spark within your self. This leaves emptiness and coldness far beyond a lack of warmth. It is a void within you that feels like a canyon that cannot be filled.

If your element of metal is weak, you can go from one guru or quest to another, always searching externally for what is missing inside you, never satisfied for long by what you find. Without the divine spark within you, it is difficult to find any value within yourself or anywhere else. You can become negative about yourself and everything you do.

A weak metal official can manifest as either of two extremes. One is the scruffiest and most unwashed person you will ever meet. The other extreme is the most thoroughly tidy and fastidious person possible. These individuals either live in squalor or try to compensate for their inner emptiness by putting up the most immaculate façade. Remember, problems show up mostly as extremes. The way these people compensate might be with ostentatious displays of gold, silver, precious stones, or material wealth to conceal the void inside.

To understand this official, it is useful to describe metal's reaction to heat. With the right amount of heat (love from the heart), metal becomes malleable. It can be shaped and used. It is flexible. It has incredible strength of form.

If we apply too much heat to metal, it loses its form. This could take the form of a child who is adored without limits, no matter what he or she does, with no consequences for dysfunctional behavior. Eventually the metal oxidizes and turns to ash. In this state it cannot hold heat or form. It is rigid and brittle. Under pressure, it no longer bends. Under stress, it shatters and fragments. The inner fire does not glow, causing the person to be cold, rigid, inert, and brittle.

When the metal element is out of balance, everything may function adequately, but the person does not seem to reach his or her potential. The word "lackluster" captures this quality best. It is as though the person performs all his or her functions without being fully engaged.

When people initially experience profound grief, they function this way. They cling to order just to get by. They need something to do, but without the divine spark, they are not really in love with what they do. There is the sense that they need to be taken by the hand, like a father would do, and be shown the way. They need direction and a connection with the wisdom of the father.

There are two things you can do to heal and purify the metal element within your self. The first is to forgive. When a painful or distasteful memory, beginning with your father (or a father figure) comes to your awareness, you need to go back to that moment in time. Conjure up all the emotional pain of that moment until it is completely real. Then, without holding anything back, give up all of that emotional pain. The more emotional pain you release, the brighter your inner light shines.

Some of what you forgive can be mean or dysfunctional actions your father (or a father figure) did. Some of the pain you remember can come from your father having to be away at work or becoming ill. Pain of loss can and should be forgiven the same way a mean action is forgiven—to release the emotional pain that gets activated every fall, or at other times when memories of father come up.

Each painful memory regarding your father that you forgive brings more purity to the element of metal within your self. With each thing you forgive, you come closer to living the true archetype of the father in your own life. It does not matter whether you are a man or a woman. Either way, the vital components of the father (metal) and mother (earth) archetypes are part of your internal makeup. Dozens of times each day you are confronted with situations where, if you have not forgiven your father and mother, you either feel bad or act out dysfunctional behavior (or, such as in my case, both).

Ultimately, you must forgive everyone who causes you pain. Forgiving the pain is like breathing out, eliminating the dregs. Then there is room for inspiration. The more you forgive, the greater capacity you have to be the lead actor in the life of your dreams.

The main way you purify and strengthen the element of metal within yourself is through abdominal breathing. Every time you catch yourself breathing shallowly and start forcefully breathing out from your lower abdomen, you awaken from a spell. As you awaken, the manner in which you consciously handle the situation allows you to replace yet another dysfunctional program. How you handle yourself after you start breathing abdominally becomes your new default response the next time a similar event happens.

It is quite normal to catch yourself breathing shallowly about twenty times a day. Replacing about twenty dysfunctional programs with conscious responses quickly builds a healthy self-esteem. Your metal shines up like a new penny.

CHAPTER 42

Large Intestine

The Official of Drainage and Dregs

Your colon keeps your blood pure and sacred. It is also responsible for eliminating the toxic thoughts, feelings, and beliefs you are exposed to during the course of each day. Many people with a sick colon official can tell the sickest jokes. When the garbage is not taken away, their minds and spirits can become pretty toxic.

If you cannot let go of (forgive) toxic mental or emotional memories, you can become a hoarder, surrounded by possessions that no longer serve any useful purpose. So, when a painful or troubling memory comes to your awareness, go inside. Conjure up all of the painful feelings of that memory until they are as real as an object you can hold in your hands. Then, give it all up. Release it. Hold none of it back.

The longer you hang on to the past, and keep dredging it up, the less space you have for the new. You have trouble moving on. You can become locked into rigid beliefs and ideas because there is no space for your new possibilities or inspiration. This rigidity can show up as frozen joint problems, mainly to the wrist, elbow, and especially the shoulder. That is the pathway of the large intestine meridian. But you can also have ankles or knees that freeze up due to holding onto old pain.

Your large intestine official propagates the right way of living, and generates evolution and change in your life. It is responsible for getting rid of the garbage. By keeping your blood pure and clean, you maintain a healthy body, a healthy mind, and a healthy spirit. Taking in and letting go are two functions that support each other and must be kept in balance.

When I was in chiropractic college, one of our professors told us that the human body could be imagined as a long tube surrounded by organs. We put food and water into one end of the tube, and wastes go out the other end. The job of the large intestine official is keeping the pathway by which we survive unblocked.

If the colon fails to get rid of the garbage, all the officials in your body suffer and cannot perform their duties. Imagine a large city with the garbage collectors on strike. That smell is similar to the smell a person has when he or she has a weak colon official.

Your skin is considered to be your third lung. If your colon official is weak, the job of offloading garbage falls to your skin. Skin diseases can be quite apparent when the colon official is not getting rid of the garbage. When your skin has to do the job, you may develop dermatitis, eczema, psoriasis, rashes, spots, or boils.

Diarrhea, the opposite problem, can be just as bad. You cannot keep anything. It all slips away too quickly. If you breathe shallowly, you may not be able to hold onto anything. It is important to breathe inspiration into your food; your breath activates it. Without adequate breath, the nourishment from the thoughts, feelings, and beliefs you are trying to take in just goes right through you, and comes out as undigested as the food from which you have gained little benefit.

CHAPTER 43

Lungs

The Official Who Receives Pure Energy From the Heavens

The amount of food you eat (from the earth, the mother) and the life energy you breathe in (from the heavens, the father) is roughly equal. The oxygen you breathe in unlocks the value of the food you eat.

Many ancient religious practices emphasized the importance of abdominal breathing as a spiritual exercise. Our culture may have forgotten how valuable abdominal breathing is, but that does not make it any less relevant to our lives.

Inspiration is the word we use for breathing, and for understanding something higher. When someone expresses a feeling such as sadness, taking a few deep breaths allows us to experience something of what that person is feeling. This opens the possibility of creatively finding the next step that needs to be taken. We connect with others through feelings.

When we experience some form of fear our unconscious response is to breathe shallow so we do not experience that fear. Breathe out forcefully. Feel the feeling. The feeling passes through your body within a few seconds leaving you free to respond with all of the clarity and power your spirit possesses.

The ancient medical treatise *Nei Jing Su Wen* describes the lungs as the "lid" of the organs. The lungs receive pure energy and send it downward. They are responsible for the downward-dispersing action as they spread their essence throughout the body.

Various forms of lung congestion are due to the lungs' inability to send energy and fluids downward. Asthma, bronchitis, emphysema, pleurisy, and upper respiratory infections can be traced back to fluids not getting dispersed downward. These are all failures in the steady rhythm and flow of taking in and letting go. If you cannot let go, you cannot take new concepts in. Often, this manifests as a person who is not even trying to make sense of what he or she is hearing. Talking to this person is like talking to a blank wall.

At the other extreme, a person with a weak lung official may be obsessed with precision and logic. They may demonstrate obsessive neatness and orderliness. They may only take in pure food and surround themselves fastidiously with the best quality materials to be found. When the metal element is weak, there is nothing that can be obtained outside of you that can fulfill your inner need to be connected to your spiritual source. Out of fear of death—fear of letting go—you may feel disconnected from your source, but the source of creation has never, ever separated from you.

When you begin to breathe shallowly, you feel cut off, separated from your connection to the source of your being. Breathe out forcefully as a habit. Your in breath is passive. Breathing out is the active part of the breathing cycle. However you breathe out is exactly how you breathe in.

Breathing abdominally is one of the seven habits that will change your life. It lets you take in the pure energy from the heavens. This way of breathing awakens you. Once you awaken, you realize that you have always been connected to the guidance and authority you desire. These qualities are within you.

CHAPTER 44

The Element of Water

The Season of Winter

Water represents endurance, the strength to carry on through hardship, and the ability to survive year after year. Healthy water reservoirs ensure that you have a future. The qualities of your water element can easily be overlooked until the system gets into trouble.

If there is too little water, you have a drought. There is little or no harvest, which creates a lot of fear about the future. Life is uncertain. There can be terrible anxieties. You have doubts about whether you can survive, much less have abundance. Life can be extremely difficult if you feel that your life has been in a drought for a long time.

Too much water causes flooding. You are overwhelmed. There is no safe place. Imagine the thoughts that run through a drowning person; terror and utter despair, the feeling of being beyond the help of fellow humans. A person in this state will not be thinking of other people. Their own self-preservation and bleak future is dominant in their mind.

Moaning or groaning indicates difficulties in the water element. A person who often moans or groans, even though his or her life does not appear any worse than anyone else's, indicates that they are either drowning or that the drought feels so severe they can see no future for themselves. Their kidney or bladder official is in distress.

Within the cycles of the seasons, water represents winter. This is a time when the earth replenishes itself with life-giving water. It is the time for going inside, for curling up by the fire with a good book. The time of darkness far exceeds the time of light.

Winter is the time to reflect on the true values of your life. Who am I? What did I incarnate into this life to do or be? What are my deep, abiding values? Am I living a life that is aligned with my value system? What are my values?

This is the time when you carefully select the seeds you will plant in the coming spring. What do I want to do with my life in the coming year? What did I leave behind this year that had value? Winter is a time for reflection.

The ears are the end organ of the water element (just as the eyes are the end organ of the liver). Kidney stress can feel like you have water in your ears. A water imbalance will often give off a bluish-black hue and puffiness around the eyes.

CHAPTER 45

Bladder

The Official Who Controls
Water Storage

Imagine a person who is responsible for ensuring that all the lakes, reservoirs, and groundwater wells in a country have enough water to last throughout all the circumstances that occur each year. This person must also protect your water levels from the effects of drought, flooding and other watery extremes. The person has to eliminate wastes by keeping enough water flowing in all the rivers. When you imagine the difficulties and challenges of this job, you get an idea of the tireless work your bladder official does for you.

If your bladder eliminates wastes too quickly and water reserves fall low, your skin and hair become dry. Your eyes and mouth get dry. If not enough wastes are eliminated, a build-up occurs and you have swelling, edema, and bloating.

Most people are chronically dehydrated, which causes 128 low-grade symptoms, none of which will kill you outright. But when you do not drink adequate quantities of the life-giving water your body needs for all of its intricate functions, your quality of life suffers. Your life force is diminished by a considerable degree. A person needs to drink a minimum of eight large glasses of water every day, more if he or she is sweating in the heat or exposed to the drying affect of the north wind. The formula is drinking half your weight in ounces of water. If you have been drinking adequate water for awhile, and do not drink enough for a couple of days, you will notice quite a few of those 128 symptoms.

Impurities and unwanted minerals must be removed or else your system is gradually poisoned. Your body, which is three quarters water, has many needs that are absolutely dependent upon your kidney and bladder officials. Your bladder official guarantees the security and future of all the other officials. Too much or too little water, and you have no future. That causes fear.

Endurance, ambition, and determination are words that represent the ability to have and maintain a healthy inner reservoir. With a healthy bladder element, your mind has fluidity. Thoughts and ideas can flow. When the bladder official is weak or sick, you might feel as though you have no (water) reserves. It is hard to think beyond the immediate difficulties.

When people are mired in desperate views and see no future, no reserves for the coming year, and can only imagine the worst possible outcomes, then their mental states can become so bleak they can loose their grip on sanity. They can begin to manifest levels of insanity as a means of escaping their desperate feelings. Suicide can become an option to someone who has no reserves, whose desperation can be too much to contemplate.

This may seem far-fetched, but there are a lot of people walking around who feel that they have no resources or that they are drowning. They can be overcome by the sheer terror of it. Their voices become monotonous, groaning and frozen, or babbling and uncontrolled.

When the water officials malfunction, the resulting distress can become all-consuming for the person. He or she may not be able to see hope anywhere. There can be an overriding urge for self-preservation or the extreme opposite. The person can seek escape from it all by constantly denying to him or herself and others that there is any danger at all. At this extreme you may often find the ultimate thrill seekers.

Water represents your feelings. Most people are just now becoming aware of the importance of their feelings. When you make it a habit to go inside and feel your feelings, they usually only last for about two seconds—then they are gone. And yet, during those two seconds, the information you garnered is usually ten times more valuable to your life than the corresponding physical and mental information put together.

Most people have not evolved beyond the mental level, which shuts them off from most of their spiritual guidance. They think their feelings; they do not actually feel them. For instance, they might say, "I am so disappointed (in a particular person)," but they do not actually go inside and feel the disappointment. Instead, they stuff the disappointment.

All those feelings that have been intellectualized but not actually felt build up over months and years, creating stagnant or polluted water in the bladder. The feelings can build to levels where you feel overwhelmed. They can make you feel like you are drowning.

Edema in the lower abdomen and legs is often due to feelings that you are not getting rid of by feeling them. As a result, your bladder is providing stagnant or polluted water to your kidneys. Your bladder grants you the ability to adapt to changing circumstances. By expressing your feelings, you do not get stuck in past events. Hanging on to old hurts keeps you trapped in the past.

Forgiveness is the most effective way to release old, painful memories. That pain will leave you for good, and your forgiveness will heal any other person involved. There is never a good reason to hang on to old hurts.

When you are aware of a feeling that is not how you want to create your world, go inside of yourself and experience it—instead of the unconscious pattern of thinking the feeling. Then ask yourself leading questions, as an agressive reporter would, to pull the depth of your spirit's wisdom to the surface. Questioning your feelings, after you have felt them, opens a pathway for the mysteries of life to reveal themselves to you. Your spiritual wisdom is latent if you do not have a vehicle for bringing that wisdom up to the level of your consciousness. Questioning why you felt those feelings is the vehicle.

CHAPTER 46

Kidneys

The Official Who
Controls the Waterways

Your kidneys and bladder work together to maintain the water supply for your body, mind, and spirit. While the bladder disposes of impurities and unnecessary minerals, the kidney makes certain the water gets to every cell in your body.

Water, as we noted earlier, equates with feelings on the emotional level. Feeling your feelings grants you access to spiritual guidance. When you pay attention, your feelings guide you around potential catastrophes in your life.

Your first feeling about anything is your spiritual preview of how that situation will play out. Your first feeling about a person you meet is how you will feel after you have known him or her for about nine months. Your first feeling about an upcoming event is how you will feel when you are actually there. Becoming aware of your first feelings deepens your wisdom. This is one of the seven habits that will change your life.

Your kidney officials do energetic work. They excel by their ability and cleverness. The cleverness described in the *Nei Jing Su Wen* is what we might call animal cunning, the innate ability to find a way around your day-to-day problems. When you are paying attention to your feelings, your cleverness comes from an immediate intuitive grasp of the situation.

A strong kidney official has a tremendous effect on your reproductive organs. Both sexual organs as well as the sperm and egg carry your body's ancestral energy. The kidney official also provides enough water so that the colon does not have to extract and save every last precious drop. Chinese humor about the kidney's role in healthy defecation observes, "When there is no water, the boat cannot sail."

In classic Chinese philosophy, the kidneys are the storehouse of ancestral energy that is passed on by your parents. This energy is different from the energy you make and use every day. It is your finest energy. When your path becomes difficult, you draw on your ancestral energy for your ultimate success.

When you push yourself to the limits of your abilities, you tap into this energy. During a powerful mental or emotional challenge, or a challenge to your spirit, you can feel more energized. You can muster clarity beyond what you normally possess. The Chinese called ancestral energy one of the "three treasures." Your spirit and *qi* (the life force that animates all life, what Westerners call the holy spirit) are the other two.

We also draw energy from the kidneys' storehouse during times of danger. The clarity of thought in those moments is profound. Your power of determination comes from this reservoir—as does your determination to take the first step on the right path.

The power of your ancestral energy deserves the utmost respect and reverence. The Chinese classics are full of dire warnings about burning your candle at both ends. When you have depleted this well, it cannot be replenished. In this depleted condition the body endures, but the mind is dull and lethargic. The spirit is all but extinguished. Long-term drug use, regardless if it is recreational or prescription, can also deplete these reserves, leaving a person listless and empty, resigned and despairing.

The kidney official creates bone and bone marrow. To the Chinese, the brain was a sea of marrow. They observed that long-term memory is a direct gift from the kidney official. *Nei Jing Su Wen* states that when the kidney is strong and full, it opens the ears, and sounds can be heard with great clarity. The mind is strong and physical energy is great.

Technically, your kidneys are emotional brains. You are a three-brain creature. You have a thinking brain up there between your ears and two feeling brains (kidneys). Each kidney contains between 15,000 and 25,000 filtration units, which are called "glomeruli." They filter 20 percent of your blood per hour for your whole life. Each of your glomeruli is completely lined with grey matter. Grey matter just happens to be the thinking portion of brain tissue. Your kidneys are intuitive brains.

Kidney logic is immediate. The instant you think about an event, your first feeling previews how you will feel when you are actually there. Your "not until you get there" brain has to predict how you will feel based upon similar events from the past. The logic of your brain is much slower and much more prone to rationalizing.

When you meet a stranger, your first impression is how you will feel about that person nine months from now. Become aware of your first feelings. They will provide you with far more wisdom and truth about what is going on in your life than what your rational mind can offer.

I do not allow my rational mind to talk me out of a first feeling about anything. Every time I have, I have paid dearly. So, ignore your first feelings at your own peril.

CHAPTER 47

Ileo-Cecal Valve

The Official Who
Guards Against Indecision

Classic acupuncture theory does not include the ileo-cecal valve as part of the kidney system, but a modern chiropractic procedure called "Touch for Health" places its function there.

Ilium and *cecum* are the old words that used to describe your small and large intestines. The valve between them is called the ileo-cecal valve.

This one-way valve only opens to accept a peristaltic evacuation from the small intestine. After the evacuation, the valve shuts tight so nothing can back up into the small intestine. The valve closing tight triggers a neurological reflex, instructing your appendix to make two squirts of mucous. In the healthy state, this valve must stay closed tight the rest of the time.

As your large intestine extracts enough of the water to firm up the wastes, the mucous from your appendix is essential to lubricate the stool. Otherwise the stool can get too hard at times and scratch the lining of your large intestine. *Your appendix is not a superfluous organ, despite what is still being taught in medical schools. Its function of lubricating the stool is invaluable.*

At the higher levels of your consciousness, this one-way check valve is about being decisive—about committing to what you know. As mentioned earlier, the three driving forces that form your character and give you purpose are cherishing people, telling the truth, and committing to what you know. Being decisive (committing to what you know as soon as you know it) is every bit as crucial to your character as cherishing others and walking your talk. It is one of the seven habits that will change your life.

When you are indecisive about the little things in your life, it is like putting a four-way stop sign where two busy freeways cross. When you have a lot of things on your mind, indecisions slow the way you process information in much the same way as viruses can slow your computer. As indecisions build up, they cloud your clarity of thinking. They slow your concentration down to a crawl. Furthermore, indecision cheapens your love and demeans your truth.

Little indecisions wreak havoc on your body. A wife might ask her husband, "What do you want for dinner?" If he answers, "Whatever," or "I don't know," his ileo-cecal valve instantly loses its tone—and it stays weak for a long time. When your valve goes soft, it allows toxic wastes from your large intestine to routinely back up into your small intestine. The toxins get absorbed into your bloodstream.

By the time the food you ate gets to the end of your small intestine, it has been about eighteen hours in transit. Your small intestine is extremely effective at extracting all of the nutrition out of it. What is left is highly toxic, but it still has the consistency of a fruit smoothie.

When indecision makes your ileo-cecal valve go soft, every time you load your abdominal muscles (which can be a hundred times a day), toxic wastes are forced back up into your small intestine. Naturally, your small intestine filters the toxic substances into your bloodstream. The toxicity overwhelms your lymph nodes, which causes your pelvis to start twisting up. This causes one side of your pelvis to twist forward, and one hip to push up higher than the other. The resulting misalignment that occurs to your whole spine and lower extremities is dramatic. And it keeps occurring as long as you are indecisive.

The high-side hip pushes the shoulder up on the same side. Your whole spine twists up and rotates. The twist in your pelvis creates misaligned vertebrae all the way up your spine. It misaligns your cranial bones. The misalignments also go downward, affecting your knees and ankles. It causes one leg to be shorter than the other. *The main cause of scoliosis (curvature of the spine) is indecision—not committing to what you know.* I bet you did not know that.

When you comprehend how incredibly expensive indecision is to your overall health, you realize that no one can afford the terrible costs of indecision. Indecision is like the wheels coming off your car.

Now the good news! When you become decisive, you wind up getting what you desire. Manifesting your desires is the easy part; figuring out what you want and then committing to it is far and away the most difficult part of the equation.

You cannot know who you are by looking at yourself, no more than you can know any other person by simply looking at him or her. You see others (and yourself) by observing the fruits of their tree.

You do not notice that you have been thinking about something until it has coalesced (i.e., built up into a complete thought form) in your mind. Then you notice that you have been thinking about this particular thing for a few days or weeks. When you become aware of something you desire to do or have, that is when you need to vote it up or down. If you decide that yes, you want to do this, then you should commit to it. Once you commit to it, your liver and gall bladder officials can make it so. Then it happens.

When you commit to a goal, fears naturally come up. If you both desire and fear something, fear will usually win out if it is not successfully confronted. You must come up with strategies that will overcome each one of your fears. If you ignore a pervasive fear, it is like turning your back on a junkyard dog. He will come up behind you and, like your fear, he will bite you.

If you do not confront your fear, it will build in intensity. Simultaneously, your courage will wilt. Soon the fear starts making what you want to do look like a bad idea. The fear wins out, and your desires go unfulfilled. Some fears are so great that it takes several strategies to successfully overcome them. Then, every time the fear comes up to your awareness, you need to focus your mind onto the strategies or affirmations that will overcome it.

Each time you review the strategy or say the affirmation(s) that effectively confronts your fear, every part of your body gets more pumped up. As you are going over your confronting thought forms, you gain further insights from your heart. By the time the feared event comes to pass, you are so pumped up that you are invincible. Nothing can stop you.

Do not allow fears to come up in your consciousness without developing plans, beliefs, or attitudes that successfully confront the fears. You must completely confront and slay the dragons if your kingdom is to remain safe.

CHAPTER 48

Living in the Material World

Having a Human Experience

The amount of time you have been in this incarnation is but a blink of the eye compared to the time you have existed as a spirit. Your spirit exists in a magnitude that is difficult to grasp. The science of quantum physics is just now beginning to grapple with understanding the physics of the spiritual realm.

Quantum physicists are finding out how difficult it is to rectify the differences between how we observe the creation we are intimately connected with, and how we as part of the Creator are the observer. We create the reality we observe. And we exist in both realms. With each new discovery, many scientists, who were previously defiant atheists, are sounding more like mystic poets. The circle of life.

We Live in an Intelligent Universe

Nature is intelligent and desires to communicate with you. Similarly, you have vast dimensions within you that await discovery. The entire elemental kingdom, which includes plants, animals, rocks, and rivers, functions as your subconscious mind.

When you accept the fact that there are no random events, the mysteries open themselves to you. If a skunk or a deer runs across the road, forcing you to slow down, the deer may be your subconscious mind telling you that you need to be a lot sweeter and gentler—that there is a lot of power in the innocence of love.[1] The skunk may be telling you to be aware of your reputation or of not casually releasing your sexual energy. Your sexual energy may need to be elevated to the level of passion for what you are doing.[2]

Your spirit's voyage of discovery is to become a pioneer, exploring the world within, discovering the subtle dimensions of your biology—then on to your spiritual dimensions. This is the new frontier. As you open up to the glories of your inner life, your current vistas become the starting point of a journey in which the world of your heart, mind, and will keeps doubling in size and glory.

To embark on this voyage of discovery, your rational mind needs to eagerly submit its will to accepting direction from your spirit. You need to make your feelings more important than your thoughts. Your feelings access the spiritual kingdom. Your body becomes like a great horse that eagerly accepts direction from a highly accomplished rider. You become the promise you have sought for so long outside of your self.

---

1   Sans, Jamie, and David Carson. *Medicine Cards: The Discovery of Power Through the Ways of Animals*. Also *Animal-Speak*, by Ted Andrews. (Llewellyn Publications, 1997.) These two books address the Native American belief that birds and animals act as messengers of the spirit world. They are communicating information to you by their presence in your life. For example, if you ran over an animal with your car, that animal gave up his life to bring his lessons to you.

2   Sexual energy is just one octave of the energy that flows from the energy center below your naval. The next octave up is passion for what you are doing. The octave above that is charisma. The highest octave of sexual energy is compassion.

How Your Spirit and Body Interface

Your spirit and your rational mind have similar goals. Neither can get what they deeply desire without being in a loving relationship with each other. Your spirit wants to fulfill the deepest desires of your heart, but your rational mind must eagerly commit to the direction of your spirit. When that happens, you wind up getting everything you ever wanted.

The body you inhabit colors all of your spirit's perceptions during this incarnation, similarly to the way a rider's perception of the ride is influenced by the qualities of the horse he rides. For example, if your body is more artistic or more athletic, it compares to riding a Morgan or an Arabian horse.

The rider's perception of the ride is profoundly affected by the horse's eagerness and committed intelligence to have a great ride. The horse must desire direction from the rider if the adventure is to be fun and fulfilling for both of them. If the horse is eager and the rider appreciative, magic happens.

I have ridden a few horses that did not want to be there. What a pain in the part of my anatomy that meets the saddle. So disappointing. I have also ridden horses that were eager for adventure, confident and sure-footed. Those rides were fun, for both of us. Both of us had fun and felt fulfilled.

Your body is the horse, and your spirit is the rider. Eager submission, eagerly giving up control to your spirit. Does that scare you? I have feared giving up control to my spirit ever since I first considered it. I think everyone struggles with control issues to some degree.

I feared I would have to give up all of the fun stuff. My fears were that being spiritual meant I would have to live some kind of ascetic life; worse, that I would have to get rid of my wildness, ambitions, and desires and become religiously correct. As it turned out, none of those fears had any substance.

Your spirit actually likes all your quirks. Some might find that hard to believe. Each of your so-called faults is like one end of a see-saw. The other end is connected to one of your genius qualities. For example, the other end of your impatience is the passion you have for life. Look at your quirks. Then imagine what the genius qualities are at the other end. Squash the fault, and you squash the genius quality. You do not want to get rid of your troublesome qualities; you just want to keep gaining better control of them.

Each ego personality has its neurotic needs and attitudes, what it fears and frets over. Your spirit accepts that. Your personality also has its genius qualities, qualities that make your life good and contribute so much to the world.

Your dimensions as a spirit are probably impossible for you to even imagine. It is for me. I am so influenced by our culture to think and perceive in certain predictable ways. I have a spiritual experience, and before even a short time I am translating it into intellectual concepts.

CHAPTER 49

You Get to Choose

You see your world exactly the way you believe it is. That is how it works. What you expect somehow turns out to be what you perceive. If you believe in lack, you get a whole lot of lack. You can have a whole lifetime, even endless lifetimes, of lack. As long as you expect lack, you will get it. If you believe in injustice, everywhere you look you will see injustice.

A good metaphor is the holodeck on the old television series, *Star Trek—The Next Generation,* the one with Captain Picard. In the holodeck, crewmembers can create a personal fantasy program. They program the exact situation they want to experience. Then they get to experience that program. The holodeck is a great metaphor for your life.

If you do not like your program, what appears to be coming at you, change what you believe. Everyone just makes his or her life up. Most people still do not realize that they can create the life they desire. Instead they create the life they do not want by continually focusing their precious attention on things they do not like, or thinking that what is should not be. Or they worry, which is fantasizing worst-case scenarios.

Worry is praying for what you do not want. This is what most people do. They read the paper, listen to the news, and talk with their friends about all of the things that have gone wrong, and all the while time is folding over on itself and creating more things that they do not like.

In the unconscious state, people spend their days and nights focusing on issues and events they do not actually want. Then, how they feel folds over to create what they are going to feel in the next block of time. Whatever they are focusing their feelings on is exactly what they are creating. Naturally, what comes at them next will feel the same way. That is why there is so much dissatisfaction in the world.

The universe is a lot like a clerk at Burger King. If you drove up to the window and said, "I want a hamburger with no lettuce, no tomatoes, no sauce, and no bun," there would probably be a pause for a moment. Then the clerk would say, "You mean you just want a slab of hamburger meat?" When you say yes, she will say, "That will be [whatever the price a hamburger is] at the window."

The clerk would not say, "Are you nuts?" She would just deliver it to you as you wish. In that same, unquestioning way, the universe delivers what you expect.

If you focus on lack, the universe gives you as much lack as you can imagine. It does not ask, "Why in heaven do you want lack?" It just delivers it to you. If you are focusing on what is going wrong, the universe, without question, delivers to you as much going wrong as you can handle. No matter what you focus your precious attention on, the universe delivers it to you without question. It is probably a good idea to focus on beauty and what you love, at least if that is what you want in your life.

The universe is like a genie in *The Arabian Nights*. No matter what you focus on, the genie says, "Your wish is my command." The power you have in the manifest world comes from a continuous stream of energies pouring out of your chakras.[1] The energy trails out behind you like the wake of a large ship. The energy unfailingly manifests both your desires and the fears you focus your awareness upon.

---

1 You have seven main chakras and a number of lesser ones. Your chakras are the organs of your most subtle body. The more loving and integrated you are, the faster the chakras spin and the clearer the rainbow-like colors they display. The energies your chakras are spinning out is encoded with all of your thoughts, attitudes and beliefs, and is amplified by your fear or love.

Put a watcher in your mind. Become aware of what you are feeling and thinking about during the day. Your feelings, what you believe, and the attitudes you are maintaining (while you are thinking about something) precisely determine what you will manifest into the world. You may have difficulty with this law, but it's the law.

Humans crave difficulty. But the difficulties do not have to be distasteful. Difficulty is not such a bad thing. Without sufficient challenges, life is boring. Although we crave difficulties, they need not be painful dramas.

We can have our difficulty play out in manifesting our splendid plans and dreams, with complexities in the planning and execution. Then, when we have overcome all of the difficulties, we experience a magnificent feeling of accomplishment.

You can create hobbies or sports or a profession that has such a steep learning curve that you will never be bored for your whole life. Everyone just makes his or her life up. You want to do it consciously, not unconsciously out of your fears.

You can work toward mastery of something you love. Your greatest joys come from having something to do that you can throw all of your passion into. That is fulfillment.

CHAPTER 50

Living 180 Degrees Out of Phase

When I was eight years old I had six intense spiritual experiences spread over a month and a half period. By the end of that period, I was left with some clarity about the natures of the conscious and the unconscious states.

I observed then (1951) that of the approximately four hundred people I personally knew, there were only two people who were actually awake. Unlike the other people I could observe, these two people continually chose love over drama. Their focus was on the goodness within and on not being judgmental. Everything about those two seemed right as rain.

Two conscious people out of four hundred represent only one-half of one percent, and this was Northern California. I figured the numbers were probably not as good in many other parts of the world. That small of a percentage is real easy to discount. When so few think like that, their perspectives are easily discounted.

I observed that people were more impressed by possessions or clothing than by inner values. If a person was nerdy or had tattered clothing, it was within societal tolerances to abuse him. Across the board, people's actions seemed intolerant.

At that time my observations were that only a trickle of people's energies went inward to the goodness within themselves. Most of their energy, as far as I could observe, went toward objects or concepts that were outside of themselves. Inner values faded into the background any time money or way of life was challenged. Most people spoke of higher values, but when it came down to what they did, things usually took precedence over inner values.

The way people related toward each other seemed backward to the direction I felt that consciousness should flow. People's value systems seemed to be turned 180 degrees opposite of what was real.

At that time, I thought there had been a terrible error. Somehow a mistake had placed me on the wrong planet. These were not my people. The meanness and intolerance everywhere was depressing to observe. From today's perspective, 1951 was an intolerant time period. Since then we have evolved a long way.

During that time my father asked me to help him when he was tuning a car in his shop. He asked me to start the car, put my foot firmly on the brake, let off the emergency brake, put the car in drive, and slowly let off on the brake so the car would creep forward. I did that, and the car crept backward. He said, "Put it in drive!" I told him it was.

He came around and stuck his head in the side window and saw that the car was actually in drive. He told me to put the car in reverse and slowly let off on the brake. I did, and the car crept forward.

He had me put the car in park and set the emergency brake. Then he said, "Turn the radio on." When I did, all we heard was real loud static. He revved the engine from under the hood. Static and the sound of pistons firing was all that could be heard through the speakers.

He had me shut the engine off. He said the distributor was in backward so the pistons were firing in reverse order. The crankshaft was rotating opposite to the normal direction. That is why the car went backward in drive, and forward in reverse.

When I asked about the radio he said, "With the pistons firing in reverse order, the electrical current to the condenser was on the wrong side of the coil. The sound of the pistons firing had already occurred before the current into the radio could be suppressed."

After he got the engine running and timed, the car crept forward when I put the transmission into drive. This time, when he asked me to turn the radio on, sweet music, beautiful and clear, came through the speakers. From that example I saw an analogy of consciousness compared to unconsciousness.

I saw that in the conscious state, most of your awareness goes inward toward your inner values. Inner values drive your thoughts and actions. Cherishing people is more important than politics, religion, or any other external concept. Really "hearing" a person who thinks differently from you is more important than being right. (Of course, like anyone else, I like to be right.)

When your awareness goes toward cherishing people and accepting what is, you spend more time in the here and now. Your spirit is at the helm of your life and your realities. You are rowing with the tide. Your presence has a liberating effect on everyone around you.

In the presence of a conscious loving person, it is easy for others to see that love really is the answer. Everything "out there" simply reflects your inner values. Your choices show others the way. When cherishing others is your motive, you tend to blaze new paths, which leave trails for others to follow. Your actions are inclusive. Unconscious actions tend to be exclusionary.

When your awareness is flowing 180 degrees in the opposite direction, positions become more important than cherishing people. Protesting what is and indulging negative feelings takes up huge blocks of time.

CHAPTER 51

Critical Mass and the Tipping Point

Willis Harmon headed up a Stanford Research Institute program during the 1970s and 1980s called the "Values and Lifestyle Study Program." They were looking for tangible signs of societal awakening. In this research project, his team looked for a time period in history that showed the greatest amount of tangible social transformative growth. The three and one-half years between 1964 and 1967 stood out dramatically in the study.

Between 1964 and 1967, there was a tremendous transformation. More than 51 million people in America changed their core values and became what Willis Harmon termed "inner-directeds."[1]

Any of us can change our attitude when we realize that it is based on inaccurate information. You can change your attitude in an instant. Values are completely different. They are deeply ingrained and usually take generations of time to change.

Becoming directed toward inner values instead of reacting to circumstances based on the values laid down by previous generations is one of the first signs of spiritual awakening. The inner-directeds in the research studies went from having outer circumstances direct their values and choices to making their choices based on inner values. This marked a radical change in how a large segment of society conducted its affairs.

---

1 Later researchers renamed this same population "cultural creatives." Most of the awakening people were from the baby boomer generation at that time.

Researchers found that this group, which was beginning to awaken, made within 10–15 percent as much money as the group that were called "yuppies" (conspicuous consumers). Instead of buying a Porsche, they bought Volvos. They invested their money in socially conscious money markets. They wanted natural-fiber clothing. They preferred watching the type of programs that led to *Discovery, Animal Planet,* History Channel, and Public Television documentaries instead of the mind-candy shows that were available at that time.

His research team sold this information to major corporations. Those corporations created whole new industries that provided this new group of consumers with what it wanted.

The awakening that first mushroomed during the late 1960s has continued to grow. Now every day in every town and city in the world, more people are awakening. You can see the signs of awakening everywhere you look. Socially conscious technology is still in its infancy, but it is starting to get a serious foothold.

I believe that human dynamics and thermal dynamics operate by the same laws. If you want to blow up a stick of dynamite, have a thermonuclear detonation or awaken enough people to ignite a movement, you must initially get 9.1816 percent of the mass to participate.

By this logic, all it takes to get everyone to wake up from the millennial slumber is for only 9.1816 percent of the total mass to awaken. That is less than ten percent of the population. 9.1816 is awakening's "critical mass."

You can see this in all kinds of organizations. To transform any group to a higher level of organization and effectiveness, you must get about 10 percent of the members behind the plan. Ten percent will vehemently oppose the plan. They represent inertia. And ten years after the change happened, the 70 percent who dragged their heels will honestly say, "I was for it all along."

All through history such a very small percentage of the worldwide population has been awake, probably less than 1 percent. When almost everyone is so unconscious and reluctant to evolve, it is difficult for such a small percentage of people to get traction. In most historical times, the inertia was overwhelming. Conscious people got ground up in the gears.

At this time in history, it feels to me like there is about five percent of the population that is becoming focused on inner values. There seems to be another ten percent that is trying to remain awake but falls back asleep more than half the time. Even though about ten percent are conscious less than half of the time, the combined 15 percent are the movers and shakers of the spiritual revolution. There is a steadily building momentum.

We do not have to wake up 70 percent to hit the tipping point. We only need to help one or two of our friends to awaken for all this to work. I find that exciting.

Throughout history the inertia of a sleeping civilization has slowed spiritual transformation down to a crawl. But, the awakening energy is now building in momentum. That momentum will quite soon hit a tipping point.[2] Once the tipping point has been reached, the ensuing rush will sweep everyone forward in its momentum.

Civilization is awakening from its historic slumber. We are rapidly approaching a moment of quantum awakening that has been foretold by all the indigenous tribes and all the religions of the world. We are now firmly in that foretold time. Time to wake up, everyone.

2 Gladwell, Malcolm. *The Tipping Point.* (Back Bay Books, 2002.)

CHAPTER 52

Above Down—Inside Out

When I attended Palmer College of Chiropractic, we learned a holistic model of health and healing called, above down—inside out. This model was the subject of considerable discussion.

Above down—inside out explains how healing works. Coincidently, this model also shows how creation works. They both operate essentially the same way. If you want to heal yourself or manifest something, this is the model. If you want to awaken from the slumber mankind has endured for so long, use the same model. Here is how it works.

A dream or plan comes into your consciousness from *above*. Similarly, a truth or an intuition also descends into your consciousness from above. When you commit to the dream or truth, you accept it *down* into your body. Then, no matter the difficulty, you manifest your dream or truth from *within* yourself *outward* into the world. This model requires courage.

Dis-ease, as you might imagine, flows in the opposite direction. Disease, which begins as dis-ease, has its origins in unconsciousness.

In the unconscious state the flow of your energies is reversed. For example, something "out there" happens. Now, because of that circumstance or action out there, you have to do things differently (outside in). Since that situation exists, you must give up your power and believe differently (below upward).

Most people unconsciously believe this model in their guts. The medical allopathic model works in this direction. Life is hard, and then you die. Every year you give up more of your physical prowess until some yucky disease drags you down and you die. Ask yourself: Is that how you want to create your world?

In the unconscious model, seeing is believing. How many times have you heard that? That model is totally based on fear. Yet, at this time in history, it is still the dominant paradigm. This model is also called "linear thinking." It is divisive. It goes all the way to critical thinking and stops just short of the next logical step of creational thinking. You must be conscious to think creatively.

There is a huge disconnect between what most people think they believe, and what they actually believe in their guts. Most think they are in control of their lives. But these same people believe that most of what they have to do is because of circumstances "out there." Because of their beliefs, they are not in control. That is reacting.

Returning to the radio analogy, when the flow of energy is backward, all you hear is the unending drama, dysfunctions, and problems created by your subconscious mind (static and pistons firing instead of sweet, clear music). The static you hear is dissatisfaction in a world where time and situations control your destiny.

By contrast, in the conscious state you can relax into the sweet, clear music of the spiritual realm. Your spirit (who you are) lives in a sea of bliss. Bliss is your spirit's natural state. Relax into who you are, and the bliss naturally bubbles up to your awareness. From the center of "now," you have access to all your spirit's connections. The turmoil of your mind ceases. Bliss bubbles up. Peace.

Seeing what you want as if it already exists starts the process of creating it into the manifest world. Put yourself in the picture. Then you have to act on intuition. You have to take the actions that your intuition points up to you. The universe likes immediate action. Delay, and the opportunities breeze right past you.

It takes an awful lot of work to stay uptight or depressed. You must keep focusing your awareness on what makes you depressed or uptight over and over again for days, weeks, and months to achieve a dependable state of depression. It takes an awful lot of work. You must be persistent for a long time to stay depressed or even to get depressed. Ugh.

There is a better way. Every part and dimension of your body functions like a polygraph. Any part of your consciousness that is out of phase with your truth is out of phase in all its functions. Out of phase works its way into being symptomatic.

Dis-ease, over time, morphs into disease. When you model the body holistically, anything that is out of phase begins to display a lack of ease or dis-ease. The body never does anything wrong. It always does the best it possibly can with what you give it.

The trouble is that when we go out of truth, we present our magnificent bodies with so many difficult compromises that our bodily functions eventually break down into disease. By contrast, it is so simple to bring the five elements, the different components of your consciousness, into balance.

CHAPTER 53

Where Is Your Focus?

You get to decide 100 percent of the time where you focus your attention. *Where your attention goes is where your creational energy flows.* Your spirit and soul must give you what you dwell upon.

There was a good example of this in *Star Trek—The Next Generation*. In that series, the ship's crewmembers had to abide by the "prime directive," which did not allow them to interfere with the social development of a primitive culture. Well, to your spirit and soul, you are the primitive culture.

Your spirit and soul are not allowed to interfere with what you choose to focus upon. In this situation the "primitive culture" is the rational mind's insistence on focusing on what it dislikes. Not only can your spirit and soul not interfere, they must give you what you keep focusing on.

If you want to spend all your time fantasizing worst-case scenarios and looping round on some highly charged but wholly insignificant issue or scene that happened, could have happened, or might happen differently, then your spirit and soul must allow that to manifest.

When you focus your feelings on what you dislike—encounters that went bad, worse-case scenarios that you fantasize might happen—those emotional experiences become the building blocks of the next segment of "reality" that you are manifesting. Put a watcher up there in your mind. Notice what you are focusing your creational energies on. Keep asking yourself, "Is this how I want to create my world?"

The lion's share of the stuff that happens to you is the inevitable consequence of your thoughts and actions. Your spirit and soul are always there injecting lessons that you must learn as part of your natural evolution. Those lessons keep happening to you until you learn them. Once you do, things like that no longer happen to you.

When you successfully deal with one portion of your curriculum, you graduate to the next. This world is not your home. Planet Earth is your training ground. You come here to learn, to master all the lessons of living in the material world. You can learn them easily or the hard way. But many believe that you will keep coming back here until you learn them. One way or another, you have to learn your lessons on this side of the veil.

Your spirit and your soul work together to create all of your life's lessons. We are precisely where we need to be to learn the lessons we need to learn. There are no accidents. Once you realize that everyone is creating his or her curriculum, it makes feeling sorry for people wrong-headed, doesn't it?

Any time you want, you can team up with a supreme being, your spirit. It has taken me a long time and many uphill gradients to yield as much control over to my spirit as I currently cede. Yet, that is what makes my life so wonderful and fulfilling.

It takes a lot of courage and conviction to surrender control to your spirit. Giving up control is scary, but hasn't almost everything you really enjoy been scary at first? Your greatest adventures begin when you submit eagerly to the lessons of your heart.

Your rational mind wants the road to be level and the boat to not rock. It wants what you believe to remain the same. When your rational mind is in charge, the faces and places may change, but the lessons remain the same. Instead of learning and moving on, you rationalize the situation and have to experience it over and over again.

A diagram of an unconscious life looks like circles that continually loop round and round. Little growth or change happens when your life goes around in circles. This is the human version of a dog chasing its tail. It looks cuter on a dog.

Your ego personality can never transcend its self-image. When you are needy, none of your accumulations or great successes can quite get you out of your "neediness." As long as your rational mind is in charge, your emotional life inhabits gradations of fear and guilt. You believe the past or future has power over you. You live in the world of time.

This is a beautiful life we live. When you choose to live in the upper limits, your life becomes richer and more wonderful every year. When you look back at the end of your life, you will have few regrets.

Living a stellar life requires less effort than it does to unconsciously struggle through the world of time. And, disciplining yourself to continually bring your focus back to what you love is infinitely more rewarding. As you begin to make these disciplines into habits, your life continues to become richer. Each year you can have a better handle on creating the world of your dreams. You are the dreamer that dreams your world into being. I wish you success and much happiness.

Seven Simple Habits
That Will Change Your Life

1) **The Inner Journey of Abdominal Breathing:** Practice breathing out forcefully from your lower abdomen. Do this every time you think of it. Do it for as long and as often as you can until it becomes your habit. Breathing abdominally keeps awakening you to the present moment. This is your first gate to heaven. It gives you the energy and courage to live the life of your dreams.

2) **Posture of Awareness:** Your posture communicates to others exactly how you expect to be treated. Correct posture allows all of your cells to communicate clearly with each other, the essence of vibrant health. It awakens you into spiritual awareness. Make your posture and gait better every year than it was the year before. Lift everything correctly, as if it was quite heavy. It's all right for you to be elegant.

3) **Walk Away From Your Injuries Like a Cat:** No limping, gimping or favoring injuries. This makes all of your injuries resolve quickly. You live and move with greater spiritual awareness. With all of your muscles participating, your movements are more joyous. This is the way of the peaceful warrior.

4) **Feel Your Feelings:** Spiritual energy and emotional energy are the most alike. Access your spiritual wisdom by going inside and feeling all of your feelings. Question feelings you have that are not how you would want to create your unique world. The answer comes from your spirit, but in your own voice. Say a resounding "Yes" to what is instead of mentally protesting it.

5) **Listen to Your "First Feelings" in New Situations:** This hones your intuition to a keen edge. Your first feelings about what you are considering doing is an exact preview of how you will feel when you actually get there. Your first feeling about a person you just met is how you will feel when you have gathered enough experiences to know that person. Trust your first feeling. Ignoring your first feeling is the triggering mechanism that lulls you into unconscious spells. Never let your rational mind talk you out of a first feeling.

6) **Cherish Others:** Your heart is the emperor of your unique world. Your heart has three main jobs: cherishing yourself, cherishing others and cherishing your plans and dreams. Everything else is a distraction. All of your cells and organs believe the thoughts you project outward are actually directed toward them.

7) **Act! Be Decisive, Make Things Happen:** It is better to make mistakes, even big ones, than to do nothing. Commit to your plans and dreams, to your truth. Allow others to know what you want, what you stand for. You might be surprised by how much help you get.

The Five Elements of Classical Chinese Acupuncture: The elements of wood, fire, earth, metal and water are the five unique channels through which we comprehend and create the world around us. Understanding the five elements allows us to take control of our thoughts, feelings, attitudes and beliefs. It helps us to better understand the world around us.

Conclusion: You and you alone create your world. There is no "out there" out there. It is all an inner game and you are the dreamer that dreams your world into being. Here are the tools. Enjoy.

Index

50, 86, 142, 179; and sports
31–33; at different elevations
32–33; in 1, 11; learning about
21–24; out forcefully 1, 4, 5–6,
77, 97, 145; shallow *xii*, 34;
with chest 11
bubbling wells 82
Buddha *xix*, 41, 55
buttocks 81, 87, 92, 120; when
walking 77–78

C

calcium 90, 91
carbon dioxide 10, 139
Carson, David 160
cat, acting like a *xv*, 56–58, 179;
compared to dog 53; moving
like a 23, 84
cecum 155
chakras 164
cherishing *xix*, 109–111, 113,
121, 168, 180
childhood 16, 17, 51, 52, 131
children 125
Chinese, ancient 112; philosophy
98
circulation sex 118–120
civilization 171
colon 143; official 144
commitment 47–50, 107, 144
communication, between body

and mind 59–60; of cells 58
consciousness *xi, xii, xx, xxii* 37,
45 114, 118, 130, 166, 168,
173, 174; awakening of 170
–171; focus of 175–176
contemplation 128, 135, 148
Core Strengthening Exercises 47
courage 176
cranial bones 157; *see also* bones
creativity 43, 122
crystals, physics of 90

D

Dalai Lama 111
danger 2
decisions 37
decisiveness *xviii*, 48, 157, 180;
lack of 108, 155–157
degenerative disc disease 91
dehydration 149
depression 131, 174
desire *xii*, 41, 61
desiccation 91
Devi, Indra 10
diaphragm 5, 10–11, 30
diarrhea 144
digestion 131
dining 128–129
disappointment 151
discipline, physical 47
Discovery 170

www.ingramcontent.com/pod-product-compliance
Lightning Source LLC
LaVergne TN
LVHW051628080426
835511LV00016B/2234